DUBAI

ENCOUNTER

LARA DUNSTON & TERRY CARTER

Dubai Encounter

Published by Lonely Planet Publications Pty Ltd
ABN 36 005 607 983

Australia	Head Office, Locked Bag 1, Footscray, Vic 3011
	☎ 03 8379 8000 fax 03 8379 8111
	talk2us@lonelyplanet.com.au
USA	150 Linden St, Oakland, CA 94607
	☎ 510 893 8555
	toll free 800 275 8555
	fax 510 893 8572
	info@lonelyplanet.com
UK	72–82 Rosebery Avenue, Clerkenwell, London EC1R 4RW
	☎ 020 7841 9000 fax 020 7841 9001
	go@lonelyplanet.co.uk

This title was commissioned in Lonely Planet's London office and produced by: **Commissioning Editor** Kerryn Burgess **Coordinating Editor** Alison Ridgway **Coordinating Cartographer** Anthony Phelan **Coordinating Layout Designer** Evelyn Yee **Assisting Editors** Charlotte Harrison **Assisting Cartographers** Anita Banh, Diana Duggan, Joshua Geoghegan, Valentina Kremenchutskaya, Sophie Richards **Managing Editor** Geoff Howard **Managing Cartographer** Shahara Ahmed **Cover Designer** James Hardy **Project Manager** Fabrice Rocher **Language Content Coordinator** Quentin Frayne **Thanks to** Glenn Beanland, Sally Darmody, Stefanie Di Trocchio, Graham Imeson, Laura Jane, Wayne Murphy, Paul Piaia, Wibowo Rusli, Celia Wood, Wendy Wright.

ISBN 978 1 74104 765 3

Printed through Colorcraft Ltd, Hong Kong.
Printed in China

HOW TO USE THIS BOOK

Colour-Coding & Maps

Colour-coding is used for symbols on maps and in the text that they relate to (eg all eating venues on the maps and in the text are given a green fork symbol). Each neighbourhood also gets its own colour, and this is used down the edge of the page and throughout that neighbourhood section.

Shaded yellow areas on the maps denote 'areas of interest' – for their historical significance, their attractive architecture or their great bars and restaurants. We encourage you to head to these areas and just start exploring!

Prices

Multiple prices listed with reviews (eg Dh10/5 or Dh10/5/20) indicate adult/child, adult/concession or adult/child/family.

> Although the authors and Lonely Planet have taken all reasonable care in preparing this book, we make no warranty about the accuracy or completeness of its content and, to the maximum extent permitted, disclaim all liability arising from its use.

Send us your feedback We love to hear from readers – your comments help make our books better. We read every word you send us, and we always guarantee that your feedback goes straight to the appropriate authors. The most useful submissions are rewarded with a free book. To send us your updates and find out about Lonely Planet events, newsletters and travel news visit our award-winning website: ***www.lonelyplanet .com/contact***.

Note: We may edit, reproduce and incorporate your comments in Lonely Planet products such as guidebooks, websites and digital products, so let us know if you don't want your comments reproduced or your name acknowledged. For a copy of our privacy policy visit ***www.lonelyplanet.com/privacy***.

LARA DUNSTON & TERRY CARTER

Australian Lara Dunston has travelled to some 60 countries but Dubai is her favourite city. With degrees in film, writing and international studies, Lara moved to the United Arab Emirates (UAE) in 1998, with husband Terry, to teach media production. She immediately fell for the place and its culture.

After fleeing Sydney's publishing industry and holding a Master's degree in media studies, Terry Carter first worked in the UAE at a teaching establishment in Abu Dhabi that was more institution than academic. After a stint as a dot-com web designer, travel writing and photography erroneously appeared a far more sensible way to earn a living. Despite this, Terry has been writing and photographing full-time ever since.

As much as Lara and Terry love modern Dubai, they find themselves increasingly drawn to 'old' Dubai, loving nothing more than wandering the Bastakiya and Shindagha Quarters, eating shwarma, and smoking *sheesha* (water pipe) in the evenings while overlooking Dubai Creek.

Lara and Terry have written four Lonely Planet guidebooks to Dubai/UAE and myriad articles on Dubai for publications including the *Independent, USA Today*, *Lifestyle+Travel* and *Paperplane*. They write about Dubai on travel blog Grantourismo (www.charlesandmarie.com/gt/). *Shukran* to everyone in Dubai who helped – you know who you are!

THE PHOTOGRAPHER

As well as writing, Terry Carter's other passion is photography. He studied photography at university, and hasn't put down a camera since. He loves shooting in the Middle East where the light, places and people are a constant joy.

Cover photograph Jumeirah Mosque reflected on a skyscraper, Digital Vision/Getty Images. **Internal photographs** p51, p61, p79, p89 by Terry Carter. All other photographs by Lonely Planet Images, and by Terry Carter except p23 Holger Leue; p41 Neil Setchfield; p12 Wayne Walton; p6, p17, p32, p116 Phil Weymouth; p71 Tony Wheeler. All images are copyright of the photographers unless otherwise indicated. Many of the images in this guide are available for licensing from **Lonely Planet Images:** www.lonelyplanetimages.com.

Deira Gold Souq glitters at night (p17)

CONTENTS

THIS IS DUBAI

Multicultural, materialistic and moving forward at a pace like no other city, Dubai is the little city-state that could. From sleepy trading port to skyscraper central, the city lives for attention and achieves it by being the very model of a tolerant Arab state in a rickety region.

As recently as 10 years ago, Dubai was considered a hardship posting for Western expats. Today they're dropping deposits on properties, keen to take part in one of the most fascinating ant farms on the planet. While this exotic destination has long been known for its Gold Souq, it's as if there were a gold rush in town, with people flocking here to make their fortunes and live the five-star lifestyle.

This is exactly what Dubai's savvy rulers envisaged when they turned their attention away from counting oil revenue to diversifying their interests to ensure that this Middle East metropolis didn't slip back into the sand. Now led by the enigmatic Sheikh Mohammed, a hard taskmaster who isn't fond of hearing *la* (no), this is a first-class tourist destination, known for its sun, sand and shopping.

While this leads many to either love or loathe Dubai, there's a fair chance that those who disparage the place as being superficial haven't left the bar of their beach resort. Head to the Heritage Village, site of Dubai's original fishing villages, where Emiratis enthusiastically practise their songs, dance and traditions, and you'll see beyond the mall culture. Spend time by the Creek, watching the *dhow* (traditional sailing vessel) traffic and the *abras* (water taxis) weave along the waterway while smoking some *sheesha* (water pipe) and you'll slip back in time. Wander the lanes of the Bastakiya Quarter or explore the multicultural neighbourhoods of Karama or Satwa and you'll experience a pleasant change from the five-star foyers. Head to the desert to see Bedouin tents and traditional practices, and you'll get a better idea of where this culture originated. Whatever you decide to do, you'll find Dubai a fascinating experiment and a city-state like no other on the planet.

Top left Latin beats rule at Tamanya Terrace (p109) **Top right** Fastest ships of the desert at Dubai Camel Racecourse (p26) **Bottom** Spectacular skyline dining along Dubai Creek (p116)

The 'sail' of Burj Al Arab rises over Jumeirah Beach (p23)

>1 DUBAI MUSEUM

'VOGUE' WITH THE MANNEQUINS IN DUBAI MUSEUM

This remarkable museum is a must-see attraction in Dubai, not only for the ancient building in which it is housed, but also for its engaging exhibits. Visitors enjoy posing with the disconcertingly lifelike mannequins in the museum's whimsical dioramas. Leading the Bedouin's beloved beast of burden seems to be the most popular photo opportunity, but try to resist playing Indiana Jones with the safari-suited archaeologists. The long-suffering guards have given up trying to stop people posing for photos with the kitsch mannequins – so fire away.

The museum's collection vividly charts Dubai's rapid progress from a tiny pre-oil fishing and pearling village – and one of the world's first free-trade ports – through to the Arabian metropolis it is today. A couple of hours spent here before exploring the rest of Dubai really helps give a sense of the city's speed of evolution.

Housed in the majestic Al-Fahidi Fort, built to defend Dubai Creek around 1787, it is the oldest building in the area. The structure is made from sea rocks and gypsum, and served as both residence to Dubai's rulers and the seat of government until 1971, when it became a museum.

In the fort's courtyard are several small wooden boats and traditional *barasti* (palm-leaf) houses, including the primitive Al Kaimah, and the summerhouse Al Areesh with traditional wind-tower *(barajeel)* 'air conditioning'. Step inside and test it out – you'll really notice the difference if visiting on a balmy day. Within the fort's walls are fascinating weapons displays featuring beautiful old silver *khanjars* (curved daggers) with camel-bone decoration, and swords inscribed with calligraphy. You'll also find exhibits on traditional Emirati dances and musical instruments. Don't miss the *shekhlelah*, a skirt hung with goat's hooves that makes music when you shake your hips.

The real treats are found in the underground museum exhibits beneath the fort, featuring a multimedia presentation on Dubai's extraordinary development through the series of dioramas brought

to life by excellent use of audio and hologramlike video projec-
tions. The vivid scenes represent life in the souq, Islam, education,
social life, architecture, costumes and jewellery, the desert and
oasis, water and survival, and – our favourite – the 'underwater' sea
exhibition.

See also p55.

HIGHLIGHTS

>2 BASTAKIYA QUARTER

GET LOST IN THE LABYRINTHINE LANES OF THE PERSIAN BASTAKIYA QUARTER

This diminutive, densely concentrated neighbourhood of tranquil, tangled lanes and wind-towered residences was once home to wealthy Persian traders, hailing mainly from Bastak in southern Iran, hence its name, Bastakiya.

Dealing mainly in pearls and textiles, the merchants were the first entrepreneurs to be enticed to Dubai by its tax-free trading and transport hub – Dubai's accessible creek was a pull long before the deep water port and airport.

Many of the elegant courtyarded buildings date to the early 1900s when the prosperous merchants constructed their homes from coral, gypsum, limestone and seashells, a step up from the more modest building material that was the ubiquitous palm tree. And this is the main reason the Bastakiya buildings have lasted – they were far more durable and valuable than the traditional *barasti* hut.

While there's some debate as to the origin of the wind-tower concept, there's no doubting they were common features of Iranian coastal buildings. The towers enabled the hot air to rise out of the building while picking up cool breezes and directing them downwards.

Now mostly restored, the Bastakiya Quarter has a lovely arty feel and as you wander the narrow, peaceful lanes you can easily imagine the life of its residents at the turn of the 20th century. Courtyard buildings you can visit include Majlis Gallery (p58), Basta Art Café (p64), XVA (p59) and Bastakiyah Nights restaurant (p64).

See also p55.

>3 SHINDAGHA WATERFRONT

ADMIRE ARCHITECTURAL WONDERS ON THE HISTORIC SHINDAGHA WATERFRONT

Take a late-afternoon or evening stroll along the evocative heritage waterfront of Shindagha at the mouth of Dubai Creek to appreciate Arabian architecture at its finest.

Several splendidly restored and reconstructed courtyard residences provide wonderful examples of wind-tower architecture, including Sheikh Juma al-Maktoum House, Sheikh Obaid bin Thani House and the most exquisite of all, the House of Sheikh Saeed al-Maktoum. Now a museum to pre-oil times, you can marvel at its architecture as well as a compelling collection of old black-and-white photographs illuminating the extraordinary history of Dubai. See p58.

Closer to the Creek's entrance are the Heritage and Diving Villages. The Heritage Village recreates Bedouin village life with *barasti* huts, a *hadheera* – a traditional seating area more primitive than a *majlis* (meeting space) – a small souq selling Arabian souvenirs, and an outdoor kitchen where burqa-clad Emirati women sit making *dosa* (flat bread). The Diving Village has displays on boat building and pearl diving, Dubai's main livelihood before the Japanese introduced cultured pearls.

In the evenings during the cooler months and Ramadan, these villages buzz with locals and visitors taking in traditional music, dance, and cultural performances and events.

Round off the evening with a relaxing meal and *sheesha* (water pipe) at Kan Zaman (p64) overlooking the magical lights of Dubai Creek. See also p118.

>4 BUR DUBAI SOUQ

TAKE AWAY TEXTILES, T-SHIRTS AND TRINKETS FROM BUSTLING BUR DUBAI SOUQ

Buzzy Bur Dubai Souq is best explored at night when it's at its liveliest. Fridays sees it crowded with expat workers on their day off, bargaining for gifts to take home, getting haircuts and buying hot Indian snacks.

The souq is loveliest in winter when cool breezes blow through the wooden arcades by the waterfront. Here, restored wind-tower buildings house shops with Russian signage selling colourful textiles, cheap T-shirts and clothes, Arabian antiques, curly-toed Aladdin slippers from Afghanistan and Pakistan, and kitsch souvenirs – this is where you come for your mosque alarm clock. Along with the alley between the Sikh Gurudaba and Hindu Shri Nathje Jayate Temple, 'Hindi Lane' (p58) – where tiny shops sell religious paraphernalia, bindis, garlands of flowers and incense, this area is the most vibrant.

Less attractive yet still appealing are the surrounding lanes of textile and sari shops, haberdashers and tailors. Nearby, Al-Fahidi St is lined with shops selling shoes, stationery and electronics – and luggage to take it all home.

See also p55 and p126.

ABRA NO.
47

>5 AN ABRA CRUISE
CRUISE DUBAI CREEK IN A CHARMING WOODEN ABRA

The heart and soul of the city is on the water amid the hustle and bustle of Dubai Creek, or Khor Dubai in Arabic. This is where Dubai keeps it real.

Hop aboard one of the open-sided *abras* (water taxis) that criss-cross the Creek, connecting Deira and Bur Dubai, to observe the action of everyday life here, and get the best views of the city. And the cheapest – the 10-minute ride costs just Dh1 or US 30¢. Expat workers use the *abras* to cross the Creek to go to work, do business, meet friends and shop, and Dubai's multicultural make-up is no more evident than on one of these little wooden boats.

If the short trip gives you a taste for more Creek cruising, you can hire an *abra* of your own from any of the *abra* stations for just Dh50 per hour (see p142). Ask the captain to take you close to the stunning white sails of the Dubai Creek Golf and Yacht Club (reminiscent of the Sydney Opera House), the swish marina at the white- and blue-domed Moroccan-style Park Hyatt (where luxury cruisers bob in the peaceful harbour), then across to verdant Creekside Park where the Creek is at its most tranquil.

HIGHLIGHTS

>6 DEIRA SPICE SOUQ

INHALE THE PUNGENT AROMAS OF FRANKINCENSE AND MYRRH AT DEIRA SPICE SOUQ

The air hanging in the old alleys of the Spice Souq is filled with the aromas of spices, herbs, nuts, pulses, dried fruits and chillies. Jute sacks overflow with frankincense and *oud* (fragrant wood), ground cardamom, cumin, cinnamon sticks and cloves, as well as local favourites, *sumac* (ground dried red berries) and *zaatar* (a mix of thyme, sumac and sesame).

The souq's wooden archways and wind towers are restored, but the market, established in the 1830s, would have an antique quality if it weren't for shops selling plastic kitchenware and toys. Focus instead on the spice sellers, taking time to stop and smell the bouquet of aromas.

The most popular buy is frankincense, from the harvested gum resin of trees in Dhofar, Oman. Emiratis burn it daily, passing it around after meals, at parties and weddings, so that the smoke perfumes guests' clothes. Traditionally bought by weight, these days the crystals are packaged in kits with a small incense burner and coal. Ask for a demo so you know how to prepare it when you get home.

See also p44 and p126.

>7 DEIRA GOLD SOUQ

BARGAIN FOR ALL THAT GLITTERS AT DEIRA GOLD SOUQ

Head to Deira's Gold Souq to haggle in the evenings when the dazzling jewellery and shimmering gems are at their most spellbinding and the wooden-latticed lanes are bustling with shoppers.

'Jumeirah Janes' (see p135) guide their visiting guests around, armed with long shopping lists, while the families of Gulf women bargain for jewellery for their daughters' dowries. In Gulf countries and the Indian Subcontinent, a good dowry is one heavy with gold. The bride is laden with ornate jewellery on her wedding day and, as tradition dictates that the gold given to a bride must be new, there's a constant flow of customers coming to the Gold Souq. The largest in Arabia, it attracts buyers from across the region and its sheer scale is impressive.

Every conceivable kind of gold and jewellery is available – from traditional to modern, cutting-edge to conservative. If you can't find it, you can always commission it.

See also p41 and p44.

>8 DUBAI CREEK DHOW WHARVES

WANDER ALONG DUBAI'S BUSTLING CREEK AND BE CAPTIVATED BY ITS CARGO-LADEN WHARVES

An amble along Dubai Creek and its chaotic wharves on a cool evening is a wonderful Dubai experience.

Small fishing villages were settled on the Creek as long as 4000 years ago, though modern Creek life traces its birth back to the 1830s, when the Maktoum branch of the Bani Yas tribe moved to the area and established a free-trade port, luring merchants from Persia.

The wharfage extends all the way from the port customs offices next to Al-Maktoum Bridge to the spice souq. The wooden *dhow* (traditional Gulf sailing vessel) boats, bound for every port from Kuwait to Iran and from Oman to India, dock here loading and unloading their cargo day and night.

A stroll along here also allows an insight into the difficult lives of the sailors who actually live on the *dhow*. The wharves are also still a focal point for small Gulf traders, showing visitors a fascinating aspect of the business. You'll see stacks of goods waiting to be transferred, including car tyres, air-conditioning units, washing machines, small cars, and even some kitchen sinks.

See also p44.

>9 SHEESHA COURTYARD

GET HEADY ON HOOKAH WITH STRAWBERRY SHEESHA AT SHEESHA COURTYARD

Smoking *sheesha* is Dubai's most relaxing traditional pastime, and palm-filled Sheesha Courtyard is the most enchanting spot to enjoy it.

Sheesha, as it's called in the Arabian peninsula, Egypt and Morocco – also known as narghile (in Turkey and the Levant) and hookah (in India and Pakistan) – is both the social act of smoking (as in 'Let's go for *sheesha*') and the long-stemmed, glass-bottomed smoking pipe that's packed with flavoured tobacco.

Dubai has some wonderful spots for *sheesha*, but nothing beats reclining on cushions under palm trees ringed with fairy lights in magical Sheesha Courtyard.

Order your pipe from a long list of aromatic flavours – our favourite is strawberry, but other taste sensations include tropical, apple, anise, grape, vanilla and even coffee. Good *sheesha* cafés, like good wine bars, pride themselves on the variety their menus offer.

If you get hooked, there are *sheesha* cafés you can try all over Dubai. Often open until well after midnight, much later during the cooler winter months when the city's population spends their night outdoors, the going rate is around Dh25.

See also p109.

>10 JUMEIRAH MOSQUE

DEBUNK MYTHS ABOUT ISLAM ON A GUIDED TOUR OF JUMEIRAH MOSQUE

Non-Muslims aren't allowed to enter mosques in Dubai, so take the opportunity to visit beautiful Jumeirah Mosque on an engaging guided visit with the Sheikh Mohammed Centre for Cultural Understanding (p35).

While the informative tours with their enlightening Q&As are the real highlight, Jumeirah Mosque is an attractive sight in itself among the cookie-cutter villas and malls of Jumeirah Beach Rd. It's a splendid example of modern Islamic architecture (building started in 1975 and was completed in 1978) with intricately detailed stonework that's especially exquisite on the two minarets. The decorative interior is also attractive.

Aimed at fostering better understanding between Muslims and other religions and cultures – something clearly needed in these times of misinformation and stereotyping – the visit introduces you to Islam and Emirati culture and allows plenty of time for you to ask questions. The organised tours run four times a week but due to their increasing popularity, it's essential to book ahead. See p35.

Visitors must dress modestly. Both men and women need to cover their arms and legs, and women are also required to wear a head-scarf. Remove your shoes before entering.

See also p71.

> 11 MADINAT JUMEIRAH

MARVEL AT THE MYTHICAL OLD ARABIAN ARCHITECTURE AT MADINAT JUMEIRAH

Pass an afternoon meandering around the mesmerising shopping, entertainment and hotel complex that is Madinat Jumeirah.

Take in the exquisite architecture inspired by ancient structures found in Saudi Arabia and Yemen, and interiors styled on old Arabian merchant houses and souqs, at the splendid luxury hotels, Al-Qasr (p113) and Mina A' Salam (p113). Venture into the winding lanes of Souq Madinat Jumeirah (p76) where you can admire the inspiring interiors while shopping for crafts and souvenirs in air-conditioned surroundings. Make sure you explore every terrace and take that intriguing staircase upstairs – you'll probably discover splendid vistas of wind towers set against the spectacular backdrop of the sprawling property. If you're staying at one of the hotels or have a restaurant reservation, catch one of the silent *abras* along the Venetian-style canals.

And when you're weary from your wanderings, there are plenty of bars and restaurants with breathtaking water views, our favourites being The Agency (p78) and Shoo Fee Ma Fee (see p78). There's also plenty to entertain you between Madinat Theatre (p82), JamBase (p81) and Trilogy (p83).

HIGHLIGHTS

>12 BAHRI BAR

ENJOY SUNSET AND THE BURJ LIGHT SHOW AT BAHRI BAR

Arrive at the colonial Arabian-style bar at least an hour before sunset to ensure you score a seat and – no matter the time of year – head straight for the vast wooden verandah. The stunning vistas are worth the trickles of sweat down your back, and if there's a balmy breeze it's simply sublime.

Once you're sinking into a comfy rattan sofa, sipping a chilled glass of white and taking in the breathtaking views – the palm-lined beach, the stunning Burj Al Arab, and mesmerising Madinat Jumeirah – you'll feel like you're on holiday, even if you're not.

And after the sun sets, when most people leave for dinner, stick around. The Burj Al Arab light show is impressive. And we're not talking about the sparkling spotlights on the curves of the building's central 'mast'. Once the sun has disappeared and the sky is black, the show begins: the whole 'sail' – dazzling white by day – is washed with colour, illuminated by over 100 floodlights programmed to create a dramatic kaleidoscopic spectacle that can be seen from all over Dubai.

See also p78.

>13 BURJ AL ARAB

SURRENDER YOURSELF TO SEVEN-STAR SERVICE AT DUBAI'S ICONIC BURJ AL ARAB

In the early 1990s ambitious Sheikh Mohammed, then Dubai's Crown Prince, knew that a world-class city – which he was determined to make Dubai – needed an icon like the Eiffel Tower. Today, there's no more fitting a symbol of Dubai than the audacious sail-shaped Burj Al Arab or Arabian Tower.

The world's tallest dedicated hotel was, at the time, the boldest of Sheikh Mohammed's projects. Construction began on the *dhow*-inspired building in 1994 – with pillars for its offshore island plunging 40 metres into the seabed – and in 1999 it opened its doors to its first awe-struck guests.

While we all marvelled at the splendid white woven glass fibre façade, we were bewildered by the gaudy 'Arabian fantasy' interior. It's as if the imagination that fuelled the extraordinary exterior ran out of puff after lifting the sail, leaving its beauty decidedly skin deep. While the interior seeks to impress with its extravagance, any taste was left at the door, and while everything that glitters *is* gold, colours matching gold are only randomly in evidence.

While the Burj was marketed as the world's only seven-star hotel, it's actually rated five-star luxury, although the staff's attentive serv-ice is seven-star standard if there was any. If you don't need to stay, opt for a treatment at Assawan Spa (p127) or a cocktail at Skyview Bar (p81) to experience service second to none.

>14 BAB AL-SHAMS & AL MAHA RESORTS

DE-STRESS AT ONE OF DUBAI'S DREAMY DESERT HIDEAWAYS

Getting out of the city to experience the desert is a must when visiting Dubai. While many settle for an organized 4WD desert safari – which *can* be fun – there's nothing like experiencing the desert over a few days at a dreamy desert hideaway.

Dubai Desert Conservation Reserve's Al Maha Desert Resort & Spa is named after the oryx it breeds so successfully. The eco-resort's luxurious stand-alone tent-roofed suites have chilled private pools and vistas of peach-coloured dunes dotted with beautiful white oryx. There are wildlife drives to see gazelles, oryx and bird-life, and sunset camel rides out to the desert where a butler awaits you with champagne. Al Maha is designed for couples, with candle-lit in-suite dining – private vehicles, visitors and children are prohibited – if you can't rekindle a romance here, it's over.

More family-friendly is the labyrinthine Bab al-Shams Desert Resort & Spa, an equally sublime desert escape. The medina-style architecture is wonderful to explore, with tiled fountains trickling in courtyards and shaded cushioned terraces lit by Moroccan lanterns. A camel awaits you on a dune beyond the infinity pool to take you on a sunset ride, while a falconry display can be enjoyed within swooping distance or from Al-Sarab bar with *sheesha* in hand. Afterwards, head to Al-Hadheerah desert restaurant for sensory overload: an Arabic band, whirling dervish, belly dancer, delicious feast and *sheesha*.

See also p122.

>15 HERITAGE HOUSE & AL-AHMADIYA SCHOOL

GET SCHOOLED ON EARLY 20TH-CENTURY LIFE AT HERITAGE HOUSE & AL-AHMADIYA SCHOOL

Get a rare glimpse inside an old pearl trader's residence at Heritage House, and learn about early education at Al-Ahmadiya School. These two traditional buildings near Deira Gold Souq offer a wonderful slice of Dubai life from the early 20th century.

Built in 1890, Heritage House belonged first to a wealthy Persian merchant before becoming the residence in 1910 of Sheikh Ahmed bin Dalmouk, a key player in Dubai's pearling industry. All rooms surrounding the spacious courtyard have been beautifully restored to represent their original function.

Adjoining Heritage House is Al-Ahmadiya School, Dubai's oldest, commissioned and funded by Sheikh Ahmed's son, Sheikh Mohammed bin Ahmed Al Dalmouk, and completed in 1912. This semi-formal school (formal education wasn't established until 1956) taught the Quran, mathematics, astronomy and calligraphy. The present Dubai Ruler Sheikh Mohammed and many of the city's key movers and shakers were among its students.

See also p41 and p44.

>16 DUBAI CAMEL RACECOURSE

**WITNESS CAMELS COMPETING IN THE LOCALS'
FAVOURITE SPORT**

While the traditional sport of camel racing was originally only prac-
tised at weddings and special events, these days it's a big business in
Dubai with races held every winter weekend from October to April.

Although there's now a small grandstand where you can watch
the lolloping camels compete, don't expect anything as fancy as
those where you view the horses at swish Nad al-Sheba. Traditionally, the action has taken place right on the track, with spectators
joining owners, as Emiratis still do now, following their lanky, long-
lashed beauties around the track in their 4WDs, urging on their pride
and joy. The rather erratic driving of the owners can be as entertaining as the camels, racing at speeds of up to 60kph.

While the use of young jockeys was once a contentious issue, now
robotic jockeys ride the ships of the desert, operated by remote control.

It's a splendid sight with the sun setting in the background behind
the camel market.

See also p88.

>DUBAI DIARY

Apart from Dubai Summer Surprises, most of Dubai's significant events are mercifully – and strategically – held in the cooler months. Along with the brilliant weather, the city has a tangibly upbeat vibe during these events as there's nothing Dubaians like more than celebrity-spotting a sports hero, a famous actor or a well-known musician at their local watering hole. See p143 for a list of holidays.

The lead pack of runners makes its way up Jumeirah Beach at the 2007 Dubai Marathon (p28)

JANUARY

Dubai Marathon

www.dubaimarathon.org

With mild January weather and one of the flattest and fastest courses in the world, this full marathon attracts a world-class field keen to set records.

FEBRUARY

Dubai Tennis Championships

www.dubaitennischampionships.com

Attracting the big serves of the top pros, the men's and women's events are a firm fixture on the tennis tours. See p128.

Dubai Tennis Championships serve up hot shots from February

A MOVEABLE FEAST

'Eid' means 'festival' in Arabic, and because Muslims follow the lunar calendar, which is about 11 days shorter than the solar calendar, Islamic holidays and eids move each year. Because the lunar calendar depends upon when the moon actually appears, these festive beginnings are hard to predict. Holidays are declared at the last minute once the Moonsighting Committee (www .moonsighting.com) confirms the moon's visibility. There are two Eids. Eid al-Fitr celebrates the end of Ramadan, the holy month of fasting, each day of which ends with Iftar, a feast to break the fast. During Eid al-Fitr Muslims buy a new set of clothes, make donations to the poor, visit family and friends and share meals and good times together. Seventy days later, Eid al-Adha, a festival of sacrifice marking the end of the Hajj, the pilgrimage to Mecca, is celebrated with the slaughter of sheep and goats and, once again, more family time and feasting!

Dubai Desert Classic

www.dubaidesertclassic.com

Luring some of the best golfers in the world to Dubai to play for some serious dirhams, this event sees expat workplace absenteeism scale amazing heights. See p128.

MARCH

Dubai International Jazz Festival

www.dubaijazzfest.com

Held over three nights, the rather eclectic programming will leave jazz aficionados sobbing – previous headliners have included jazz-free combos such as TOTO and Supertramp.

Dubai World Cup

www.dubaiworldcup.com

Dubai's racing season culminates in the world's richest horse race, but with no betting, attention turns to the loony fashion free-for-all of the punter. See p128.

JUNE

Dubai Summer Surprises

www.mydsf.com

The greatest trick this city ever pulled was to convince the world to shop here, while every resident with enough money for a plane ticket flies to a destination more liveable than Dubai in summer. Still, at this time of year the hotels are discounted and the roads are quiet.

OCTOBER

UAE Desert Challenge

www.uaedesertchallenge.com

This desert rally is the penultimate round of the FIA Cross Country Rally World Cup. Held over four days, there's a special spectator stage in Dubai.

Diwali

Lights, candles and firecrackers highlight this magical festival of light that brings together the ever-growing community of Indian expats in Dubai.

DUBAI DIARY

Glitz and glam on the red carpet at the Dubai International Film Festival

DECEMBER

Global Village

www.globalvillage.ae

Starting in mid-December, running till mid-February, this event showcases cultures from around the world – not to mention some serious shopping at the pavilions of the myriad nations represented.

Dubai Shopping Festival

www.mydsf.com

Kicking off in late December and lasting through to the end of February, this festival dedicated to maxing out credit cards sees live music, performances, fireworks every night and hotels having 100% occupancy. Being a shopping festival, it can take hours to get to a mall because of the traffic.

Dubai International Film Festival

www.dubaifilmfest.com

Dubai's week of stargazing is a hit for its excellent Middle Eastern programming and a miss for its obsession with B-list celebrities and bad Hollywood premieres. See p138.

Dubai Rugby Sevens

www.dubairugby7s.com

One of the biggest events on the sporting and social calendar, this Bacchanalian orgy of tackling and tippling now hosts over 30,000 spectators for the final day. See p128. Book ahead.

A belly dancer wiggles her stuff at a desert safari (p122)

ITINERARIES

ONE DAY

Life in Dubai has always centred on the Creek, so spend your day on the historic waterfront. Start with breakfast at Sheikh Mohammed Centre for Cultural Understanding (p35) then explore the Bastakiya Quarter (p12). Cool down at leafy Basta Art Café (p64) before browsing Bur Dubai Souq (p14). Time your visit to the air-conditioned Dubai Museum (p11) for the hottest part of the day, then in the late afternoon hire an *abra* (water taxi) for a Creek cruise (p15). In the evening explore Deira Gold Souq (p17), Spice Souq (p16) and Shindagha (p13) then dine at Kan Zaman (p64) or Bastakiyah Nights (p64).

THREE DAYS

Do the one-day itinerary but leave Deira and its souqs for day two. Start with shopping and people-watching at Deira City Centre (p40) followed by lunch. Relax at the poolside before heading out at 5pm to visit Al-Ahmadiya School (p25) and Heritage House (p25), then haggle in the Gold Souq (p17), Deira Covered Souq (p41) and Spice Souq (p16). Wander the *dhow* wharves (p18), then freshen up back at your hotel and head out for dinner to Verre by Gordon Ramsay (p50) followed by drinks at The Terrace (p52). Next day, visit Jumeirah Mosque (p20) followed by shopping at Mall of the Emirates (p92) and snow at Ski Dubai (p98). Refuel at Emporio Armani Caffé (p94) or Almaz by Momo (p93). Taxi it to Madinat Jumeirah (p21) for the architecture and shopping, followed by sunset at Bahri Bar (p22). Have dinner at Tagine (p107), *sheesha* (water pipe) at Sheesha Courtyard (p19) and drinks at The Rooftop (p108).

FIVE DAYS

Follow the three-day itinerary then stay a couple of nights at a desert resort (p122) or do a desert safari (p122). If you opt for the latter, check out Snapshots (p122) for ideas. Art lovers could spend an afternoon at Dubai's galleries. Shopaholics should revisit the souqs to pick up a carpet and buy some gold or browse Ibn Battuta Mall (p101), BurJuman Centre (p60) and Karama Souq (p62). On the final night, enjoy a Creek dinner cruise (p68).

Top left Take time out in the courtyard of Basta Art Café (p64) **Bottom left** A world of movies at Deira City Centre (p46)

BUDGET DUBAI

It costs nothing to explore the Bastakiya Quarter (p12), Shindagha (p13), souqs (p126) and shopping malls (p125), Dubai Creek and *dhow* wharves (p18). Most museums and galleries are free or cheap, such as Dubai Museum (p11). During the cooler months walk around Deira and Bur Dubai, catch an *abra* across the Creek, and take the bus to Jumeirah. A tasty shwarma and fresh juice make a great cheap eat, but if you want alcohol with your meal check *What's On* and *Time Out Dubai* magazines for lunch, buffet and all-you-can-eat deals, as well as happy hour and drink promotions.

STAYING COOL

During the warmer months when temperatures climb into the 40s (Celsius), take taxis everywhere. Spend your days in air-conditioned comfort at Dubai Museum (p11), shopping malls (p125) and spas (p127). Hit the

Snowboarding heaven at Ski Dubai (p98)

FORWARD PLANNING

If you're planning to be in Dubai from November to March (the busiest period) book your hotel (p112) and desert resort (p122) as far in advance as possible.

Three weeks before you go: reserve a table for dinner at Gordon Ramsay's Verre (p50; info .creek@hilton.com); sign up for invitations to art exhibition openings at galleries The Third Line (art@thethirdline.com), B21 (www.b21gallery.com) and XVA (www.xvagallery.com); and register for the weekly newsletter to find out about (and buy tickets online to) concerts, theatre, musicals, comedy and sporting events at Time Out Dubai tickets (www.itp.net/tickets/). Clubbers should sign up for newsletters to see which international DJs will be in town at 9714 (www.9714.com), Mumtazz (www.mumtazz.com) and Platinum List Dubai (www.platinum listdubai.com).

One week before you go: email the Sheikh Mohammed Centre for Cultural Understanding (smccu@emirates.net.ae; www.cultures.ae) to reserve places at its cultural breakfast and guided visit to Jumeirah Mosque (p20); book yourself in for a spa treatment (p127); and reserve a table for dinner at Tagine (p107) or Maya (p106).

The day before you go: book your desert safari (p122); and get yourself on the guest lists for the hottest club events at Platinum List Dubai (www.platinumlistdubai.com).

snowy slopes at Ski Dubai (p98) or get wet at Wild Wadi Waterpark (p83). Don't attempt to walk anywhere until the evening, when you can explore the souqs (p126), Bastakiya Quarter (p12) and Shindagha (p13), but even then continually drink water to rehydrate. If you insist on sun, don't worry, it won't take long to get that tan, so hit the beach or pool in the morning and late afternoon.

DURING RAMADAN

During the holy month, Dubai's streets are dead during the day, people work shorter hours and it's not possible to eat, drink, chew gum or smoke in public. At night, the city comes alive as people break the fast together after sunset at the evening meal of Iftar. Non-Muslims join Muslims at Iftar tents for Arabic food, *sheesha* and traditional music (check the local magazines for Iftar promotions). Plan on spending your days by the hotel pool and spa, then heading out for Iftar, after which you can hit the sights, souqs and malls. Shopping is a popular Ramadan activity and malls stay open until after midnight. Note that while people are night owls during Ramadan, picnicking in parks, smoking *sheesha* in cafés and chilling out in Iftar tents, nightclubs close for the month, there's no live entertainment, and while alcohol is served in Dubai, the rest of the UAE is dry.

A *dhow* wharf worker takes an afternoon ride along the waterfront

NEIGHBOURHOODS

This Arabian metropolis grows at a mind-boggling pace and while multiple-lane thoroughfares make zipping around Dubai a breeze out of rush hours, during peak periods those same roads jam with traffic – so it makes sense to explore the city one neighbourhood at a time.

Dubai's myriad neighbourhoods do have names, but most aren't in every-day use – telling your taxi driver you're staying at 'Tawi as Saigh' will get a blank stare. We've therefore condensed many tiny neighbourhoods into five larger areas: Deira, Bur Dubai, Sheikh Zayed Rd, Jumeirah and New Dubai.

Deira and Bur Dubai make up the old centre with most of the action focused on Dubai Creek, which divides them. Chaotic Deira covers the souq areas of Al-Ras, Al-Sabkha and Naif; the Rigga eat street; and Al-Garhoud, the area between Deira City Centre mall, Al-Garhoud Bridge and the airport. Cross the Creek south to Bur Dubai in an *abra* (water taxi) or via Al-Shindagha Tunnel, Al-Maktoum Bridge or Al-Garhoud Bridge.

Historic Bur Dubai takes in the area south of the Creek to Al-Dhiyafah St, from the port to Al-Garhoud Bridge, including Al-Shindagha, Al-Bas-takiya, Al-Karama and Oud Metha.

Architects' playground Sheikh Zayed Rd begins at Trade Centre Roundabout heading southwest to Interchange No 5. Here we include industrial Al-Quoz, home to an increasing number of art galleries, Nad al-Sheba racecourse and camel racetrack, and Ras Al-Khor.

The spine of sprawling Jumeirah is resort-laden Jumeirah Beach Rd, starting at eat street Al-Dhiyafah St and running parallel to the coast for about 16km to Al-Sufouh Rd near Madinat Jumeirah. The area stretches inland a few big blocks, taking in residential neighbourhoods including Umm Suqeim and Al Safa.

The new, ritzy, rapidly growing area known as New Dubai begins on Sheikh Zayed Rd around Interchange 5, extending a few kilometres along Abu Dhabi Rd as far as Ibn Battuta Mall and Jebel Ali, and toward the coast to Dubai Marina.

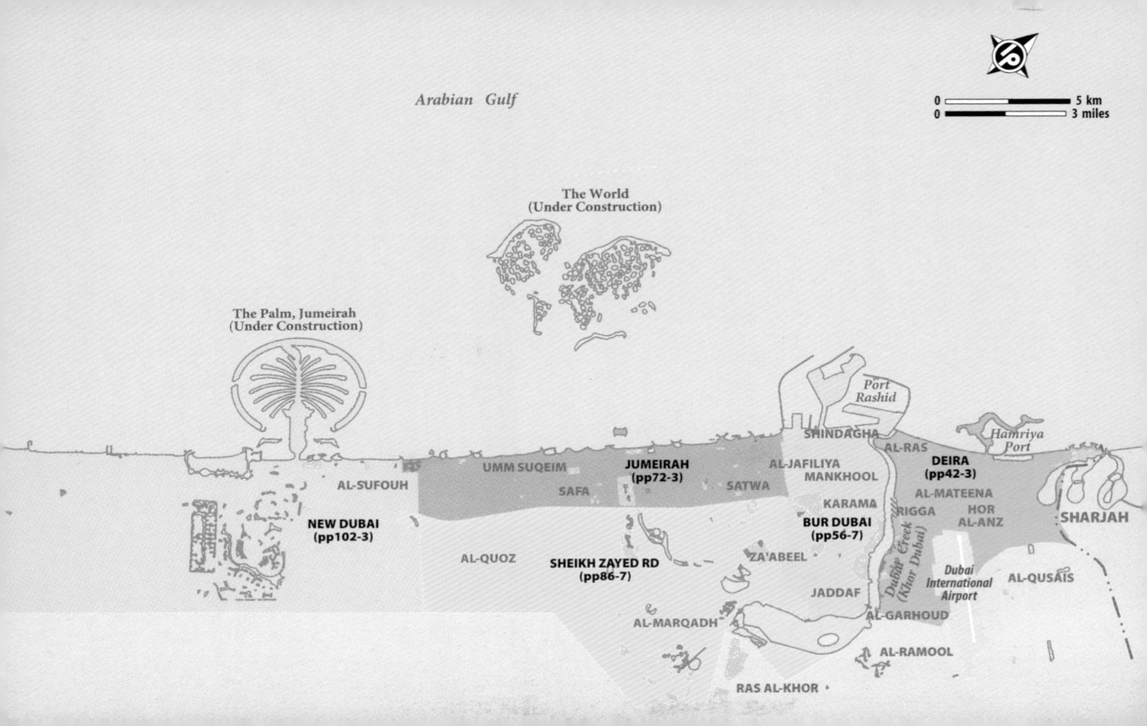

Arabian Gulf
0 5 km
0 3 miles
The World
(Under Construction)
The Palm, Jumeirah
(Under Construction)
Port
Rashid
Hamriya
Port
SHINDAGHA
AL-RAS
DEIRA
(pp42-3)
AL-MATEENA
HOR
AL-ANZ
RIGGA
SHARJAH
UMM SUQEIM
JUMEIRAH
(pp72-3)
SAFA
SATWA
AL-JAFILIYA
MANKHOOL
KARAMA
BUR DUBAI
(pp56-7)
AL-SUFOUH
NEW DUBAI
(pp102-3)
AL-QUOZ
SHEIKH ZAYED RD
(pp86-7)
ZA'ABEEL
Dubai Creek
(Khor Dubai)
Dubai
International
Airport
AL-QUSAIS
JADDAF
AL-GARHOUD
AL-MARQADH
AL-RAMOOL
RAS AL-KHOR

> DEIRA

Deira is home to most of Dubai's souqs and *dhow* wharfage, always buzzing with activity and a fascinating place for a walk in the evenings. Busy Baniyas Sq, also known as Al Nasr Sq, is Deira's centre. Just off Baniyas Rd, the National Bank of Dubai is a beautiful sight at sunset. The neon-lit surrounding streets are excellent if you're shopping for carpets or electronics, especially Al-Sabkha Rd, which is also a great place for a quick snack with several good shwarma and hot chicken shops. Also wonderful for a stroll on a cool winter's night is Al-Mateena Rd, with its palm-filled central reservation and dozens of kebab restaurants.

DEIRA

◉ SEE

Al-Ahmadiya School	1	A1
Deira Covered Souq	2	B2
Deira Gold Souq	3	B1
Deira Spice Souq	4	A1
Dhow Wharves	5	B5
Heritage House	6	A1
Naif Souq	7	B2
Perfume Souq	8	B1

⬒ SHOP

Ajmal	(see 10)	
Al-Ghurair City	9	C4
Al-Jaber Gallery	(see 10)	
Carrefour	(see 10)	
Deira City Centre	10	B7
Magrudy's	(see 10)	

Mikyajy	(see 10)	
Rituals	(see 10)	
Virgin Megastore	(see 10)	
Women's Secret	(see 10)	

🍴 EAT

Café Chic	(see 14)	
China Club	11	B3
Chopstix	12	C3
Glasshouse Mediterranean Brasserie	13	B4
M's Beef Bistro	14	C8
Miyako	15	C1
More	16	C8
Shahrzad	(see 15)	
Thai Kitchen	17	B7
Verre by Gordon Ramsay	(see 13)	
YUM!	(see 11)	

▼ DRINK

Café Havana	(see 10)	
Irish Village	18	B8
Ku Bu	19	B3
Terrace, The	(see 17)	

★ PLAY

Cinestar	(see 10)	
Dubai Creek Golf & Yacht Club	20	A7
iBO	21	C8
QD's	(see 20)	

Please see over for map

SEE

☀ AL-AHMADIYA SCHOOL
☎ 226 0286; Al-Ahmadiya St, near Gold Souq; ⏰ 8am-8pm Sat-Thu, 2.30-7.30pm Fri

In an exquisite courtyard house with gorgeous decorative gypsum panels, Dubai's oldest school was built in 1912 by Sheikh Mohammed bin Ahmed bin Dalmouk. Students paid a few rupees to attend, with the Sheikh sponsoring poorer students, a practice that continues today. See p25.

☀ AL-MAMZAR PARK
☎ 296 6201; Al-Mamzar Park; per person/car Dh5/30; ⏰ 8am-10.30pm Sat-Wed, 8am-10.30pm Thu-Fri

Tranquil Al-Mamzar Park, with its white sand beach, has splendid views across the still water to Sharjah. On a small headland on the outskirts of Dubai, this is a hidden gem. There's a swimming pool as well as changing rooms, barbecues, and chalets for rent. Women and children only Wednesdays.

☀ DEIRA COVERED SOUQ
Between Al-Sabkha Rd, 67 St & Naif Rd

Deceptively large and disorienting, don't be surprised if, just as you think you have a handle on where you are, you get lost all over again. This warren of narrow lanes is lined with small shops selling everything from lurid textiles to plastic coffeepots – but if you get worn out by the shopping, just take in the captivating surroundings.

☀ DEIRA GOLD SOUQ
On & around Sikkat al-Khail St, between Souq Deira & Old Baladiya Sts

The Gulf's glitziest gold market is impressive, but once you're done gawking at the jaw-dropping displays, grab a bench on the main drag to absorb the street action. You'll see Afghani guys

Dazzling shopping adventures at Deira Gold Souq

30B

17C
2B

D 80

6C

44B
42A

Salahuddin Rd

44A
36

E 11

12C
20A

21
23

13A

2A
11A
14

9A
10A

11B
13B

D 78

12A
7A

3C

Al-Ittihad Rd

5B
9B

22A
22B

6

Abu Bakar al-Siddiq Rd

DNATA
Airline Centre

26C

Clock Tower
Roundabout

Al-Rigga
Post Office

Avis

40C

Hertz
Budget

6B
1S

13

9

12B

D 85

Deira City
Centre

10

RIGGA

Al-Maktoum Rd

Baniyas Rd

Al-Maktoum Bridge

D 81

Riyadh St

Dubai Creek

(Khor Dubai)

Airport Rd

47

4A

16

Al-Garhoud Rd

D 11

Park Hyatt
Dubai

17

Dubai Creek Golf
Course

E 89

14

Al-Bustan
Rotana

35

25

25A

AL-GARHOUD

Garhoud Rd

14

18

Dubai Tennis
Stadium

Dubai
International
Airport

Al-Garhoud Bridge

5

6

7

8

F

E

D

shifting impossibly heavy carts, and colourfully-caftaned African ladies haggling for the glittery stuff. See p17.

GOING FOR GOLD

Deira Gold Souq is considered to be the best in the world – that means the cheapest gold but with the highest quality and widest range. Gold is sold by weight in Deira Gold Souq, but there's room to bargain. The cost of a piece of gold jewellery varies depending on its grade, whether it's handcrafted or machine-made, and how much work has gone into the design. When you find a piece you like, continue to shop around, compare prices, and if you see a similar piece elsewhere, attempt to get the price down. If a salesperson tells you a piece is 22 carat, you can be sure it is, as there are strict authenticity laws in place.

◙ DEIRA SPICE SOUQ
Between Baniyas Rd, Al-Sabkha Rd & Al-Abra St Deira
Do your olfactory senses a favour at this tiny aromatic market – inhale the pungent scents from the sacks brimming with herbs and spices. When you're done playing 'guess which spice is in that sack' with the shopkeepers, take in the wind-tower architecture and take away some souvenirs: saffron, frankincense and rosewater.

◙ DHOW WHARVES
Baniyas Rd
The wooden *dhows* that ply the Arabian Sea and Indian Ocean have docked at Dubai Creek since the 1830s, when the Maktoums established free trade to lure merchants away from Persia. Our favourite winter pastime is an evening stroll along the wharves. See p18.

◙ HERITAGE HOUSE
☎ 226 0286; Al-Ahmadiya St, near Gold Souq; ⏲ 8am-7.30pm Sat-Thu, 2.30-7.30pm Fri
Get a glimpse inside a wealthy pearl merchant's former residence and enjoy the kitsch dioramas at this elegant courtyard house. Built in 1890 it belonged to Sheikh Ahmed bin Dalmouk, whose son established Al-Ahmadiya School next door. Note there's no wind tower here; before the surrounding buildings were constructed, its open verandahs captured the cool sea breezes.

◙ NAIF SOUQ
Between Naif South St, 9a St & Deira St
More like a typical Middle Eastern bazaar than Deira Covered Souq, Naif Souq is where Emiratis and African expats like to shop for everything from fake Chanel *shaylahs* (women's headscarves) to cheap kids' clothes. Although

WORTH THE TRIP: HISTORIC SHARJAH

Al Sheyoukh and Al Maraija are two tiny neighbourhoods of **Sharjah** (8km out of Dubai's city centre) that have been extensively rebuilt, restored and pedestrianised in recent years to become the Heritage Area (well-signposted, off Burj Ave, close to the Corniche). A number of interesting little museums in this historic precinct come under the umbrella of **Sharjah Heritage Museum**. The former Al-Naboodah family home has a beautiful courtyard and fascinating displays of clothing and jewellery while the **Sharjah Islamic Museum** has a collection of coins from around the Islamic world, handwritten Qurans, and Turkish, Syrian and Afghani ceramics. Many of the museums don't have English signage, but they're free and are definitely worth a quick look.

this is mainly a clothes souq, you will also come across stalls that sell bags or kids' toys. Sometimes more interesting than the shopping is the amazing insight this souq gives into the lives of the locals.

◉ PERFUME SOUQ

Gold Souq, on Sikkat Al-Khail St

Several blocks of perfume shops near the Gold Souq hardly warrants the title 'souq', yet these bustling stores sell a staggering range of Arabic *attars* (spicy Arabic perfumes), *oud* (fragrant wood) and incense burners. More fascinating than the perfumes is the perfume-buying ritual – just watch the burqa-covered ladies waft the smoke from burning *oud* under their *abayas* (Islamic women's dress) as they sample the pungent aromas.

SHOP

⬚ AJMAL *Cosmetics*

☎ 295 3580; Deira City Centre, Al-Garhoud Rd; ☼ 10am-10pm

The place to buy traditional Arabic perfumes, Ajmal is always crowded with local ladies in elegant burqas, who love coming here to stock up on jewel-encrusted bottles of exotic oils.

⬚ AL-GHURAIR CITY

Shopping Mall

☎ 223 2333; corner Al-Rigga & Omar ibn al-Khattab Rds; ☼ 10am-10pm

This is a one-stop-shop for Emirati national dress: stylish *abayas* and *shaylas*, quality leather sandals, and *dishdashas* (traditional men's robes) in chocolate brown and slate grey (popular in winter). Other shops worth browsing specialise in Arabian perfumes and Indian embroidery.

▢ AL-JABER GALLERY
Arts, Crafts & Souvenirs
☎ 295 1010; Deira City Centre, Al-Garhoud Rd; ⏱ 10am-10pm
It may be touristy but this cluttered store has the largest selection of Arabian souvenirs and handicrafts around. Not all are from the Middle East, but those Indian cushion covers will help complete that Asian look when you get back home, while a henna kit and *sheesha* pipe should trigger memories of your trip to Dubai.

▢ CARREFOUR *Supermarket*
☎ 295 1600; Deira City Centre, Al-Garhoud Rd; ⏱ 9am-midnight Sat-Thu, 10am-midnight Fri
Perpetually crowded Carrefour, the city's cheapest supermarket, has the best selection of international products, delicious fresh bread, Arabic pastries, Iranian caviar, cheeses from around the globe and barrels of delicious Middle Eastern olives – perfect provisions for a picnic down by the water.

▢ DEIRA CITY CENTRE
Shopping Mall
☎ 295 1010; Al-Garhoud Rd; ⏱ 10am-10pm
This is still Dubai's most popular mall, despite openings of bigger and brighter malls such as Ibn

Battuta (p101). City Centre has an excellent range of shops, the best bookshop (Magrudy's), Carrefour supermarket, food courts, cinemas and an amusement centre. Avoid the horrendous taxi queue by walking a block in any direction and hailing one from the road.

▢ MAGRUDY'S *Bookshop*
☎ 295 7744; Deira City Centre, Al-Garhoud Rd; ⏱ 10am-10pm
The best English-language bookshop in the city (even after the opening of Borders), Magrudy's has glossy souvenir coffee-table books, great reads on Middle East history, politics and culture, the latest fiction and a terrific travel section, but for magazines head to Carrefour.

▢ MIKYAJY *Cosmetics*
☎ 295 7844; Deira City Centre, Al-Garhoud Rd; ⏱ 10am-10pm Sat-Thu, 2-10pm Fri
Girls, don't leave Dubai without buying some Mikyajy make-up. This Gulf brand's enormous local popularity is due to its vibrant colours, made for Middle Eastern skin tones, but the vivid cosmetics brighten up any face. Buy the 'Starry Nights' kit before hitting the clubs in Dubai.

WORTH THE TRIP: SHOPPING SHARJAH'S SOUQS

Arsah' means a large open space, originally a stop for travellers, and the courtyard in delightful old **Souq Al-Arsa**, located off Burj Ave, **Sharjah** (about 8km out of Dubai's centre), keeps that tradition alive. The *areesh* (palm frond) roof and wooden pillars make it more traditional in feel than most Dubai souqs and there's a great coffee shop where you can hang with the locals. But it is a fabulous place to shop with more authentic Arabian antiques and curios than you'll find in Dubai. The **Blue Souq** on Corniche Rd is also worth a look for Bedouin jewellery and carpets.

◈ RITUALS *Cosmetics*

☎ 294 1432; Deira City Centre, Al-Garhoud Rd; ☽ 10am-10pm

These terrific natural products from the Netherlands are based on turning tedious routines into meaningful rituals. How could you not take to dishwashing in a woody-scented liquid called Bamboo Treasure or enjoy ironing with Lotus Mist? Lingering in a luscious bath of Magic Milk could work for you too. They also sell travel-sized selections.

◈ VIRGIN MEGASTORE
Music & DVDs

☎ 295 8599; Deira City Centre, Al-Garhoud Rd; ☽ 10am-10pm

Virgin's enthusiastic staff will happily suggest some souvenirs from their huge offering of Middle Eastern sounds, from Oriental lounge to *khaleeji* (popular Gulf). There's also a decent selection of Arab and Iranian DVDs and a great range of MP3 players, including iPods.

◈ WOMEN'S SECRET *Fashion*

☎ 295 9665; Deira City Centre, Al-Garhoud Rd; ☽ 10am-10pm

This sassy Spanish label specialises in funky, sexy and affordable lingerie, swimwear and sleepwear inspired by global styles and pop culture.

◈ EAT

◈ CAFÉ CHIC

Fine Dining $$$$

☎ 282 4040; Le Méridien Dubai, Airport Rd, Al-Garhoud; ☽ 12.30-2.45pm & 8-11.45pm; Ⓥ

Overseen by Michelin-starred chef Philippe Gauvreau, this elegant restaurant (forget the café nomenclature) has lifted its game. Classics such as homemade fois gras terrine and more adventurous fare, such as tagine lobster, are cooked to perfection and beautifully presented. Surprisingly for a French restaurant, even vegetarians get a brilliant degustation menu. The signature chocolate soufflé remains a decadent delight.

⊞ CHINA CLUB
Contemporary Chinese $$$
☎ 222 7171; InterContinental Hotel, Baniyas Rd; ☽ 1-3pm & 8-11pm
This gorgeous warm red space whispers refined Chinese restaurant and delivers it in spades. Whether you choose a booth or one of the sexy banquet rooms, make sure you stick to the classics such as the note-perfect Peking duck, which outshine the contemporary dishes on offer. Want more? Come back for Friday yum cha.

⊞ CHOPSTIX
Chinese/Indian $$
☎ 272 0000; Marco Polo Hotel, Al-Mateena St; ☽ 1-3pm & 8pm-midnight
The surprise package of this unassuming four-star hotel, chef Richard and his attentive staff serve up classic Chinese dishes alongside more creative dishes inspired by his mother's cooking. Try the salty flavour sensation of his crackling spinach, devour some salt and pepper squid, and don't miss his crispy chilli potatoes.

The best of Chinese and Indian cuisine at Chopstix

🍴 GLASSHOUSE MEDITERRANEAN BRASSERIE

Modern Mediterranean $$$

☎ 227 1111; Hilton Dubai Creek, Baniyas Rd; ☾ 12.30-3.30pm & 7-11.30pm

It's not easy growing up with a more famous sibling, however, despite being just across the way from the excellent Verre (p50), the Glasshouse has really come into its own. The more focussed brasserie menu, with takes on classics such as salad niçoise, is exemplary and there's an excellent by-the-glass wine list.

🍴 MIYAKO *Japanese* $$$$

☎ 209 1222; Hyatt Regency, off Al-Khaleej Rd; ☾ 12.30-3pm & 7-11pm

Revamped as part of the old Hyatt's makeover, this consistently outstanding Japanese restaurant has style to match the flavours on offer. Tuna and salmon are reliable options for the sushi and sashimi, but there are far more tempting choices on offer – try the crumbed fried oysters and *kakuni* (braised pork belly).

🍴 MORE *Café* $$

☎ 283 0224; near Welcare Hospital, Al-Garhoud; ☾ 7.30am-12.30am

For city-dwellers craving that relaxed local café vibe, More fits the bill. Long communal tables are stacked with magazines and there's wi-fi for those who can't leave home without their Mac-Book. While the bo-ho feel and excellent coffee and *zaatar* (Middle Eastern thyme) tea are welcome, the food can be hit and miss.

🍴 M'S BEEF BISTRO

Steakhouse $$$$

☎ 282 4040; Le Méridien Dubai, Airport Rd, Al-Garhoud; ☾ 12.30-2.45pm & 7.30-11.45pm

The key to running a good steakhouse is developing a solid clientele, the kind who come in at least once a week – M's has a cabinet filled with personal engraved knives for its regular guests. Classics dominate; try the beef carpaccio or beef tartare (prepared tableside). The aged (six-weeks) tenderloin and the fabulous Wagyu are also winners.

🍴 SHAHRZAD *Persian* $$$$

☎ 209 1200; Hyatt Regency, off Al-Khaleej Rd; ☾ 12.30-3.30pm & 7.30-11pm, closed Sat

Shahrzad offers excellent Iranian cuisine and live music surrounded by antiques evoking the feel of old Persia. As soon as you enter the restaurant the enticing aromas of bread baked in the traditional *tanour* (oven) and meat kebabs slowly cooking on the open grill will make your mouth water.

NEIGHBOURHOODS

DEIRA

V

☎ THE THAI KITCHEN *Thai* $$$
☎ 602 1234; Park Hyatt Dubai; ⏱ 7pm-midnight, brunch 12.30-4pm Fri
You'll find this stylish restaurant a worthwhile trip to northeastern Thailand, once home to chef Khun Supathra (one of Dubai's only female chefs). Try the tangy, refreshing pomelo or green papaya salads as well as the beef with hot basil, then down one of the fabulous spicy cocktail creations.

☎ VERRE BY GORDON RAMSAY *Fine Dining* $$$$
☎ 212 7551; Hilton Dubai Creek, Baniyas Rd; ⏱ 7pm-midnight
Dubai's most consistent fine dining experience is Gordon Ramsay's Verre. While Mr Ramsay appears to thrive on swearing at people on TV, his Dubai outpost remains true to what earned him his Michelin stars. Don't expect crazy culinary fireworks – Ramsay's forte is fine ingredients, French technique and smooth service (see opposite for an interview with Verre sommelier Luca Gagliardi).

☎ YUM! *Noodle Bar* $$
☎ 222 7171; InterContinental Hotel, Baniyas Rd; ⏱ noon-1am
The Radisson's answer to Noodle House (p94), Yum! serves up far-Eastern fare fresh from its open kitchen. The *tom kha gai* (chicken and coconut soup) and wok specials such as *char kway teow* (stir-fried noodles) are excellent.

Yum! dishes up perfect Asian noodles

Luca Gagliardi
Chef Sommelier, Verre by Gordon Ramsay

Where do you eat on your day off? Tang (p107) for highly creative cuisine; Certo (p104) for the most authentic Italian pizzas (the chef's Italian!); and Bella Donna (p77) for excellent products, attentive service and relaxed atmosphere. **Favourite drinking spots?** Trilogy's rooftop (p83), gorgeous people, magical setting; Buddha Bar (p108), best cocktails and it's always buzzing; Tamanya Terrace (p109), great views and *sheesha*. **Best thing about Dubai?** There aren't too many headaches compared to other major cities. **Why should people visit?** To experience the most globalised city in the world. **Your tips?** Treat yourself to a spa, go fishing, do a desert safari, ski at Emirates Mall, but whatever you do, don't go inside Burj Al Arab!

NEIGHBOURHOODS

DEIRA

> **WORTH THE TRIP: ARTY SHARJAH**
>
> **Sharjah** (about 8km out of Dubai's city centre) has a remarkable Arts Area (well-signposted, off Burj Ave) that is worth checking out for the splendid heritage architecture alone, but the excellent **Sharjah Art Museum** houses the UAE's finest art collection, including Orientalist paintings and provocative contemporary art – as you'd expect from a museum that hosts the cutting-edge Sharjah Art Biennale (p123). It also has a stylish café that does decent light meals.
>
> Around the peaceful main square opposite the museum are a number of arts centres, including the **Emirates Fine Arts Society**, which displays work by local artists, and the **Very Special Arts Centre**, a workshop and gallery for disabled artists.

DRINK

CAFÉ HAVANA *Café*
☎ 295 5238; Level II, Deira City Centre, Al-Garhoud Rd; 🕒 8am-midnight

The city centre's most popular café, this sprawling, stylish place provides a rare chance for visitors to hang out with the local Emirati guys who kick back here for hours.

IRISH VILLAGE *Irish Bar*
☎ 282 4750; Aviation Club, Dubai Tennis Stadium, Al-Garhoud Rd; 🕒 11am-1.30am

The beer garden at this Irish pub with its kitsch façade is popular with expats. The after-work crowd packs the place on Thursday nights, but the weekend sees a more relaxed bunch lazing on the grass by the 'lake' with the ducks and a Guinness or three.

KU BU *Cocktail Bar*
☎ 205 7033; InterContinental Dubai Hotel, Baniyas Rd; 🕒 7pm-3am

Kick back with a few cocktails while nodding to some funky tunes provided by the house DJ in this intimate bar with an Afro-cool interior and secluded seating areas that are concealed by plush drapes.

THE TERRACE *Lounge Bar*
☎ 602 1234; Park Hyatt Dubai; 🕒 noon-late

With the boats bobbing on the water nearby and a DJ in the evenings spinning chill-out grooves, this waterside lounge bar specialises in vodka, champagne, caviar and oysters. What a wonderful place to while away a few indulgent hours on that last night in Dubai. Head here earlier in the trip and you'll be making plans to stay.

PLAY

⭐ CINESTAR *Cinema*

☎ 294 9000; Deira City Centre, Al-Garhoud Rd; Dh20 before 6pm, Dh30 after 6pm
Catch the latest Hollywood blockbusters, American indie flicks and the occasional European film at this popular state-of-the-art 11-screen complex.

⭐ DUBAI CREEK GOLF & YACHT CLUB *Golf Club*

☎ 295 6000; www.dubaigolf.com; near the Deira side of Al-Garhoud Bridge; per 18 holes Thu-Sat Dh600, per 18 holes Sun-Wed Dh500
Designed by golfing legend and former Dubai Desert Classic winner Thomas Björn, this gently undulating, palm-shaded golf course on the creek is the city's sexiest. Its location next to the Park Hyatt Dubai (p113) makes it even more attractive for golf junkies who can walk to the golfing green.

⭐ IBO *Club*

☎ 398 2206; Millennium Airport Hotel, Al-Garhoud Rd; ⏰ 8pm-3am
With its laidback attitude, mixed crowd and chic retro interior – disco ball, velvet sofas and shagpile rugs – iBO remains our favourite Dubai club. It keeps regulars coming back for some of the most interesting DJs from around

Tee off in style at Dubai Creek Golf & Yacht Club

the globe, along with indie movie nights and special events.

⭐ QD'S *Bar*

☎ 295 6000; Dubai Creek Golf & Yacht Club; near the Deira side of Al-Garhoud Bridge; ⏰ 6pm-3am
This open-air bar overlooking Dubai Creek is a sublime spot for *sheesha* and beers during the cooler winter months, particularly on a moonlit night, when the Creek looks especially magical.

> BUR DUBAI

Bustling Bur Dubai is home to the restored historical quarters of the Bastakiya & Shindagha, wonderful for late afternoon and evening strolls. Bur Dubai Souq is just as lively as the Deira Souqs, although its wooden arcades and waterfront location make it more pleasant. Little India, in the surrounding streets, with its textile and sari stores, Bollywood tape shops and Indian eateries, can easily absorb a couple of interesting hours. Past the concrete jungle of Golden Sands is Karama, home to a popular souq with cheap souvenir shops and counterfeit designer goods. The neighbourhood may be made up of dilapidated low-cost housing but it has a real community spirit that's hard to find elsewhere in Dubai.

BUR DUBAI

◉ SEE
Bastakiya Quarter	1	E2
Bur Dubai Souq	2	E2
Dubai Museum	3	E2
Heritage & Diving Villages	4	E1
Hindi Lane	5	E2
Majlis Gallery	6	E2
Sheikh Saeed al-Maktoum House	7	E1
XVA	8	E2

⌂ SHOP
Allah Din Shoes	(see 2)	
Al-Orooba Oriental	(see 9)	
Amzaan	(see 12)	
Bateel	(see 9)	
BurJuman Centre	9	D3
Etro	(see 9)	

Faces	(see 9)	
Five Green	10	D5
Gift World	(see 11)	
Karama Souq	11	C5
Wafi City Mall	12	C7
Wafi Gourmet	(see 12)	
Whistles	(see 9)	

🍴 EAT
Asha's	(see 12)	
Awtar	(see 20)	
Basta Art Café	13	E2
Bastakiyah Nights	14	E2
Kan Zaman	15	E1
Lemongrass	16	C6
Manhattan Grill	(see 20)	
Mumtaz Mahal	17	E2
Peppercrab	(see 20)	
Thai Chi	(see 12)	

🍸 DRINK
Cooz	(see 20)	
Ginseng	(see 12)	
Vintage	(see 12)	

★ PLAY
Blush	(see 12)	
Cleopatra's Spa	(see 12)	
Creekside Park	18	E6
Dubai Creek Cruises	19	F3
Grand Cineplex	20	D8
Movies Under the Stars	(see 12)	
Peanut Butter Jam	(see 12)	
Za'abeel Park	21	B4

Please see over for map

SEE

◉ BASTAKIYA QUARTER

**Between Bur Dubai waterfront,
Al-Musallah Rd and Al-Fahidi St**
With its labyrinthine lanes lined
with traditional wind-tower
architecture, the old Bastakiya
Quarter on the waterfront east of
Bur Dubai Souq is a magical place
to explore. See p12.

◉ BUR DUBAI SOUQ

**Between Bur Dubai waterfront and
Al-Fahidi St**
Wander through this vibrant
textile souq on the waterfront and
experience the hustle and bustle
deep within its wooden-latticed
arcades. See also p14.

◉ DUBAI MUSEUM

☎ 353 1862; **Al-Fahidi St, opp Grand
Mosque & Diwan; adult/child Dh3/1;**
⌚ **8.30am-8.30pm Sat-Thu, 3-9pm Fri**
The museum's manageable size
and entertaining exhibits give
you a quick and comprehensive
introduction to Dubai's history,
culture and traditions. Apart
from the kitsch dioramas and
disturbingly lifelike mannequins,
highlights include finds from Al-
Qusais archaeological site dating
back to between 2500 BC and 500
BC. Explanations are provided in
Arabic and English. See also p11.

Football fun in the Bastakiya Quarter

◉ HERITAGE & DIVING VILLAGES

☎ 393 7151; **Al-Shindagha Rd;** ⌚ **8am-
10pm Sat-Thu, 8-11am & 4-10pm Fri**
The delightful Heritage and
Diving Villages provide a great introduction to traditional Bedouin
coastal village life. The cooler
winter evenings see more locals
than tourists passing through for
the traditional performances and
activities, such as rifle-throwing
competitions broadcast on local
TV. See p13.

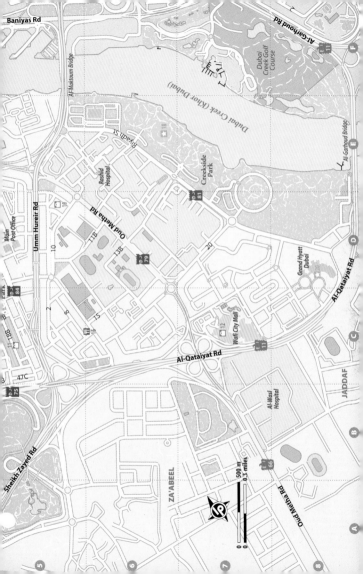

'HINDI LANE'
Behind Grand Mosque, off Ali bin Abi Talib St

Two modest places of worship, the Hindu Shri Nathje Jayate Temple and the Sikh Gurudaba, are hidden away behind the Grand Mosque. In a tiny alley that runs between them, known as 'Hindi Lane', vendors sell religious paraphernalia and temple offerings – fruit baskets, flower garlands, gold-embossed holy images, sacred ash, sandalwood (for burning) as well as packets of bindis.

MAJLIS GALLERY
☎ 353 6233; Al-Fahidi Roundabout; ⏲ 9.30am-1.30pm & 4-7.30pm Sat-Thu

In a charming courtyarded house in the historic Bastakiya Quarter, the city's oldest commercial gallery, established in the 1970s, exhibits paintings, Islamic calligraphy and sculpture by Dubai-based artists, along with high quality locally produced pottery, ceramics, glassware and handicrafts.

SHEIKH SAEED AL-MAKTOUM HOUSE
☎ 393 7139; Al-Shindagha Rd; adult/child Dh2/1; ⏲ 8.30am-9pm Sat-Thu, 3-10pm Fri

Garlands of sacred marigolds shine along 'Hindi Lane'

BARGAINING 101

Relished by some, tedious for others, bargaining in souqs can get you a 20% to 50% discount if you're prepared to haggle. Do as the locals do: when you are offered a price, suggest 50% less. Use your gut instinct to respond to the trader's reaction, adjust your offer accordingly and then as the process draws to an end, ask for their final and best price. If they agree to your offer, pay up. Offering a lower figure or worse yet, leaving, may be considered extremely impolite. Bargaining in a mall is acceptable if you are in carpet, computer and electronics stores. Perfume and cosmetics stores will sometimes also offer discounts.

This elegant 30-room courtyard-ed house is worth a visit as much for its gorgeous architecture as its engaging exhibits from Dubai's pre-oil days and fascinating old black-and-white photographs. Built in 1896 during the reign of Sheikh Maktoum bin Hasher al-Maktoum, the house was the Maktoum residence until the death of Sheikh Mohammed's grandfather, Sheikh Saeed, in 1958.

🎬 XVA

☎ 353 5383; www.xvagallery.com; **behind Basta Art Café, Al-Musallah Roundabout;** 🕑 **9.30am-8pm, closed Fri**
This beautifully restored Bastakiya building is home to one of Dubai's best contemporary art galleries with frequently changing exhibitions, a fabulous little shop, courtyard café, and stylish boutique hotel (p112) upstairs.

 # SHOP

🏠 ALLAH DIN SHOES
Arts, Crafts & Souvenirs

☎ 050 515 4351; Abra dock; 🕑 **10am-10pm Sat-Thu, 4-10pm Fri**
This small outdoor stall near the *abra* (water taxi) dock was the first to offer fabulous sequinned slippers and gold-thread curly toed Aladdin shoes from Pakistan and Afghanistan. Although everyone's selling them now, it's still the best for quality and variety.

🏠 AL-OROOBA ORIENTAL
Arts, Crafts & Souvenirs

☎ 351 0919; BurJuman Centre; 🕑 **10am-10pm Sat-Thu, 2-10pm Fri**
This is one of Dubai's few stores to stock authentic antiques and quality collectables. It has an impressive selection of Bedouin jewellery, old *khanjars* (curved daggers), beautiful ceramics, miniature Persian paintings and carpets.

🏠 AMZAAN *Fashion*
☎ 324 6754; Wafi City Mall, Al-Qataiyat Rd, near Al-Garhoud Bridge; 🕙 10am-10pm Sat-Thu, 2-10pm Fri

This funky boutique belonging to charming Sharjah princess Shaikha Maisa al-Qassimi (opposite) is one of our favourites, stocking edgy brands like Free for Humanity, Manoush, Religion Cycle, Pause and Faust, and Dubai-based labels you won't find elsewhere. Don't leave town without buying something from Dubai's Pink Sushi (opposite).

🏠 BATEEL *Food*
☎ 355 2853; BurJuman Centre, cnr Khalid bin al-Waleed & Trade Centre Rds; 🕙 10am-10pm Sat-Thu, 2-10pm Fri

Bateel applies European chocolate-making techniques to quality local dates to produce the most delicious date chocolates, truffles, marzipan and nougat, along with date jams and a sparkling date drink. Offering dates is intrinsic to traditional Arab hospitality, but now Emiratis offer silver platters of Bateel's wrapped chocolate dates at parties and celebrations.

🏠 BURJUMAN CENTRE
Shopping Mall
☎ 352 0222; cnr Khalid bin al-Waleed & Trade Centre Rds; 🕙 10am-10pm Sat-Thu, 2-10pm Fri

BurJuman is Dubai's most glamorous mall with a swanky Saks Fifth Ave, floors of exclusive boutiques stocking everything from haute couture to more affordable designers, elegant jewellery stores and French cafés.

🏠 ETRO *Fashion*
☎ 351 3737; BurJuman Centre, cnr Khalid bin al-Waleed & Trade Centre Rds; 🕙 10am-10pm Sat-Thu, 2-10pm Fri

Jetsetters love Italian designer Giacomo Etro's exuberant designs, inspired by his journeys and the connections he makes between disparate symbols and cultures. His imaginatively exotic collections have featured everything from textured ponchos to mirrored skirts.

🏠 FACES *Cosmetics*
☎ 352 1441; BurJuman Centre, cnr Khalid bin al-Waleed & Trade Centre Rds; 🕙 10am-10pm Thu-Sat, 2-10pm Fri

Faces stocks those brilliant niche perfume and cosmetic brands, previously impossible to find in Dubai, that women used to travel to Paris for. Serge Lutens, L'Artisan Parfumer and Annick Goutal – cancel that flight, they're all here.

🏠 FIVE GREEN *Fashion & Art*
☎ 336 4100; Aroma Garden Café Building, Oud Metha; 🕙 10am-11pm Sat-Thu, 4-11pm Fri

This edgy boutique and art space owned by siblings Shahi and

Shaikha Maisa al-Qassimi
Artist, Photographer and Owner of Amzaan (opposite)

Describe Dubai's fashion scene. It's growing. Dubai's Fashion Week at Bur-Juman (opposite) was great, all haute couture, with Valentino, Ungaro, Lacroix; it's better with the big Paris fashion houses. **Your favourite local designer?** Pink Sushi's Raghda Bukhash. She's taken our culture and tradition and given it a postmodern twist. Also 'Ice Lolly', an Emirati guy who does great printed T-shirts with Swarovski crystals. **Best thing about Dubai shopping?** You can find any brand you want, brands from all over the world, everything's here. **Apart from Amzaan, best place to shop?** Harvey Nichols, and my friend's shop, Bauhaus (p101), at Ibn Battuta Mall – she stocks Missoni sports! **Favourite mall?** Wafi City, for quality and tranquillity, it's more relaxing than the other malls. **Shopping tips?** Mall hop, shop around, but get out of the malls too, Dubai has many interesting tiny little stores.

Shehab Hamad (see interview, p79) sells unisex urban streetwear from Paul Frank, GSUS, XLarge, BoxFresh and Upper Playground, along with Dubai-based designers Saadia Zahid, Mona Ibrahim, chadiyo and Essa. Here you will also come across idiosyncratic shoes by Irregular Choice and Acupuncture, Etnies sneakers, Lomo cameras, as well as indie mags and music.

GIFT WORLD
Arts, Crafts & Souvenirs
☎ 335 8097; Block T, Karama Shopping Centre, Karama; 9am-10.30pm Sat-Thu, 4-10.30pm Fri
There's little space to move in this wonderfully cluttered Aladdin's Cave. You'll bump your head on Moroccan lanterns and Syrian hanging lamps as you rummage through the Oriental bric-a-brac for that unique piece of Bedouin jewellery or search stacks of sequinned bedspreads for that perfect colour.

KARAMA SOUQ
Arts, Crafts & Souvenirs
18B St, between 33B & 45B Sts, Karama
Savvy shoppers and lovers of kitsch (Burj Al Arab paperweight, anyone?) save their souvenir shopping for Karama. It's cheaper than the malls and those keen on under-the-counter designer

fakes will welcome the repetitive call of 'copy watches, copy bags, Madam'. (You'll also find counterfeit sports gear and teenage streetwear here.)

WAFI GOURMET *Food*
☎ 324 4555; Wafi City Mall, Al-Qataiyat Rd, near Al-Garhoud Bridge; 10am-10pm Sat-Thu, 2-10pm Fri
Dubai's best deli has glass counters displaying delicious Arabian delicacies – juicy olives, pickles, peppers and cheeses, freshly made hummus, muttabal and tabbouli, and great Lebanese pastries. During the cooler months, call in here, make up a mezze plate and head down to the Creek to join the local families picnicking.

WHISTLES *Fashion*
☎ 351 5070; BurJuman Centre, cnr Khalid bin al-Waleed & Trade Centre Rds; 10am-10pm Sat-Thu, 2-10pm Fri
This whimsical women's fashion label, only available in the UK, Denmark and the Middle East, is incredibly hard to resist. Recent collections have exhibited eclectic influences from the 1960s and 1970s, and all display wonderful attention to detail, from fine embellishments to exquisite tailoring.

EAT

ASHA'S
Contemporary Indian $$$

☎ 324 4100; Pyramids, Wafi City Mall, Al-Qataiyat Rd, near Al-Garhoud Bridge; 🕐 12.30-3.30pm & 7.30pm-2am

With its informed service, funky décor and contemporary takes on traditional Northern Indian cuisine, Asha's has spawned a few copycats in Dubai. It's still the leader of the pack and while traditionalists are well served, it's best to take a walk on the wild side here.

AWTAR *Lebanese* $$$$

☎ 317 2222; Grand Hyatt Dubai, Al-Qataiyat Rd 🕐 7pm-3am Sun-Fri

Perhaps Dubai's best take on the Lebanese-style 'big night out', Awtar serves up lashings of mezze, aromatic meats and good vibrations provided by the band and belly dancer. Take the Lebanese lead and arrive at 10pm, order up a feast and prepare not to be hungry for a couple of days afterwards.

New Indian flavours at Asha's

NEIGHBOURHOODS

BUR DUBAI

THE PERFECT SNACK

Arguably the best fast food ever invented, the shwarma is *the* staple snack food of the Middle East. Although it has different names in other countries – gyros in Greece and döner kebab in Turkey – it's only known as shawarma in Dubai (or shwarma, shawerma, chawerma, but let's not get too pedantic). While the Greeks might disagree, this hand-held meal originated in Turkey, where döner literally means 'one that turns', referring to the vertical rotisserie the shawarma meat is cooked on. Strips of marinated meat (usually chicken or lamb) and fat are placed on a huge skewer that rotates in front of a grill. Dubai is blessed with an enormous number of shwarma joints; Al Mallah (p76) is one of our favourites. But the rule is to eat at any that are busy; they always offer the freshest.

🍴 BASTA ART CAFÉ *Café* $
☎ 353 5071; Al-Fahidi St, Bastakiya;
🕐 10am-8pm
An ideal refuelling stop if exploring the Bastakiya Quarter, this leafy courtyard café in a traditional wind-tower building attracts a loyal local following who head here for Farah's refreshing Basta Specials (fresh lime and mint juice) and big salads – the grilled haloumi, asparagus and mixed lettuce combo is deservedly popular. It also does delicious breakfasts and offer a healthy kids' menu.

🍴 BASTAKIYAH NIGHTS
Arabian $$$
☎ 353 7772; Near the Rulers Court, off Al-Fahidi St, Bastakiya; 🕐 12.30pm-midnight Sat-Thu, 2pm-midnight Fri
Situated in a restored house in the Bastakiya Quarter (p12), this restaurant takes full advantage of its location by offering a taste of

traditional Arabian food through its set or à la carte menu (though no alcohol is served). Romantic private rooms and open seating on the roof create a unique Dubai dining experience.

🍴 KAN ZAMAN *Arabic* $$
☎ 393 9913; Heritage Village, Al-Shindaga; 🕐 11am-3am
A trip to Heritage Village is incomplete without a visit to this creekside favourite. During the cooler months, the sprawling outdoor area is the place to leisurely sample mezze and grills, and watch the passing parade of boats. Afterwards, loosen up with some apple *sheesha* – an obligatory way to end the meal.

🍴 LEMONGRASS *Thai* $$
☎ 334 2325; near Lamcy Plaza;
🕐 noon-midnight; V
An independent favourite of expats, the excellent (and satisfy-

ingly hot) traditional Thai cuisine keeps the doors swinging and the delivery guys busy. The Lemongrass set (a selection of starters for two) is obligatory. Salads and curries are also popular here. You must save room for the sago. No alcohol served.

MANHATTAN GRILL
Steakhouse $$$$
☎ 317 1234; Grand Hyatt Dubai, Al-Qataiyat Rd; ☾ 7.30-11.30pm, closed Fri
It is an accomplishment that this stylish eatery manages to feel so very New York in a hotel that has *dhow* (traditional Gulf sailing vessel) hulls plastered to the ceiling.

The food lives up to its stylish surroundings, too, with sensational steaks, juicy and perfectly cooked to order. Sides of mash and vegetables compliment them well.

MUMTAZ MAHAL *Indian* $$
☎ 351 9111; Arabian Courtyard Hotel, Al-Fahidi St; ☾ 7.30pm-2am
One of our favourite North Indian eateries, the tandoor specialities, excellent service and in-house Indian band and dancers make for a fun night out. While any of the smoky-flavoured specials that comes out of the clay oven is excellent, we especially love the lamb dharba masala.

Tasty tandoor and good vibrations at Mumtaz Mahal.

NEIGHBOURHOODS

BUR DUBAI

🍴 PEPPERCRAB
Singaporean $$$$

☎ 317 2222; Grand Hyatt Dubai, Al-Qataiyat Rd; ⏰ 7-11.30pm Mon-Sat, till 1am Wed & Thu

The busy open kitchen and huge fish tanks are almost a tourist attraction in their own right, but the fresh fish and shellfish are the real draw at this smart restaurant. The signature chilli-pepper crab is sublime, but there are plenty of innovative creations on the menu as well.

🍴 THAI CHI
Contemporary Thai & Chinese $$$

☎ 324 4100; Wafi Pyramids, Wafi City Mall, Al-Qataiyat Rd, near Al-Garhoud Bridge; ⏰ noon-3pm & 7.30-midnight; ♿ Ⓥ

What could be a muddle of pan-Asian plates is saved by the separation of the Thai and Chinese kitchens and menus. The Thai staples are well executed and if it's Chinese you're after, the Peking duck is a must.

Extraordinary seafood creations in the open kitchen at Peppercrab

Live jazz couldn't get smoother at Cooz bar

Y DRINK

Y COOZ *Cocktail Bar*

☎ 317 1234; Grand Hyatt Dubai, Al-Qataiyat Rd; ⏱ 7pm-2am

Sip a martini at this dimly lit, super-stylish cocktail bar and enjoy some smooth live jazz – some of the most authentic jazz sounds in Dubai in fact – by the resident jazz singer and pianist.

Y GINSENG *Lounge Bar*

☎ 324 8200; Wafi Pyramids, Wafi City Mall, Oud Metha Rd; ⏱ 7pm-2am Fri-Wed, 7pm-3am Thu

This funky Far Eastern–themed bar with Chinese murals on its walls serves up the best *caiparinhas*

(national drink of Brazil) in the city and some excellent drink deals, including cocktails, during happy hour from 7pm to 9pm daily. Soak it up with some spicy Asian tapas.

Y VINTAGE *Wine Bar*

☎ 324 0000; Wafi Pyramids, Wafi City, Oud Metha Rd; ⏱ 6pm-1.30am

Aficionados love the extensive wine list here. Vintage's wide range of grape by the glass – including 'wine flights' (four different tasting glasses) – and delicious cheese plates win us over, while others swear by the fondue. Makes a great pre-dinner meeting spot.

PLAY

⭐ BLUSH *Dance Club*

☎ 324 8200; Wafi Pyramids, enter via Ginseng; Dh60; 🕐 10pm-3am Thu

Blush attracts a more down-to-earth crowd than most clubs to its weekly nights of funky house featuring a wide range of well-known DJs, from Blush impresario Dion Mavath to Ministry of Sound favourite Mark Knight. Email Dion (info@clubblush.net) in advance to get on the guest list.

⭐ CLEOPATRA'S SPA *Spa*

☎ 324 7700; www.cleopatras-spa.com; Wafi City Mall, Al-Qataiyat Rd, near Al-Garhoud Bridge

Dubai's first day spa is still considered to be its best. There's a bewildering array of facials, massages, baths and wraps. Guys aren't left out either – while your better half is experiencing Cleopatra's Ritual (Dh966), you can try Anthony's Anti Stress package at the Male Spa, although at Dh1133 it's hardly going to soothe the impact of the bill.

⭐ CREEKSIDE PARK *Park*

Dubai Creek, Bur Dubai; admission Dh5; 🕐 8am-11pm Sat-Wed, 8am-11.30pm Thu, Fri & public holidays, women & children only Wed

This oasis of palm-shaded green stretches from Al-Garhoud Bridge towards Al-Maktoum Bridge,

making for a heavenly escape from the heat and humidity of Dubai's streets. There are children's playgrounds – as well as the outstanding Children's City – kiosks, eateries, a cable car, an amphitheatre and beaches (though swimming in the Creek is not recommended).

⭐ DUBAI CREEK CRUISES *Cruise*

Al-Seef Rd, Bur Dubai side of the Creek; 🕐 varies

If your *abra* trip (see p15) gives you a taste for more Creek cruising, consider a chic fine dining experience on sleek Bateaux Dubai (www.bateauxdubai.com), or a buffet and bellydancing cruise on a traditional *dhow* or modern catamaran with Danat Dubai Cruises (www.danatdubaicruises.com).

⭐ GRAND CINEPLEX *Cinema*

☎ 324 2000; Grand Hyatt Dubai, next to Wafi City Mall; admission Dh25-30

At this hi-tech 10-screen multiplex showing the latest English-language movies, you'll also find an array of cafés, DVDs and music, and an ATM to get cashed-up after spending all your dirhams.

⭐ MOVIES UNDER THE STARS *Cinema*

☎ 324 4100; Wafi City Mall Rooftop, Al-Qataiyat Rd; 🕐 8pm-late; admission free

There's something for all the family at Za'abeel Park on the weekend

On Sunday nights during the cooler autumn, winter and spring months, you can sink into a beanbag, plunge your hands into some big boxes of popcorn and enjoy themed outdoor film nights.

⭐ PEANUT BUTTER JAM
Live Music
☎ 324 4100; Wafi City Mall, Al-Qataiyat Rd; 🕑 4-7pm Fri, except summer
During the cooler months on Friday nights (call to make sure) you can settle into the same beanbags (see opposite), enjoy a barbeque buffet and watch local bands play live acoustic sets. You can even join them for a jam session.

⭐ ZA'ABEEL PARK *Park*
☎ 800 900 (Dubai Municipality); Sheikh Khalifa bin Zayed Rd & Al-Qataiyat Rd
This fantastic 51-hectare park has gentle undulating green hills (perfect for picnics), gorgeous lakes and ponds, a low-impact jogging track, excellent sports facilities and kiosks – not to mention fabulous views of the Sheikh Zayed Rd skyline. It gets wonderfully packed on weekends.

> JUMEIRAH

This beautiful stretch of coast with its namesake road running parallel to its white sand beach is home to Dubai's best beach resorts. It's also Dubai's most interesting residential area, dirt-poor in the dilapidated neighbourhoods bordering Satwa, and middle- to upper class from Jumeirah Mosque to Umm Suqeim. Turn off Jumeirah Rd to have a snoop around: the midsize villas are mostly rented by big organizations for their managers (their 'ladies-who-lunch' wives have received the expat label 'Jumeirah Janes'). The largest villas are home to more affluent Emirati families with Sheikhs' palaces occupying the prime beachside real estate. To service local residents there's an increasing number of chic eateries and shopping malls. This area is also home to Dubai's most remarkable construction projects, including Burj Al Arab (p23) and the man-made island developments of The World and The Palm, which can be seen from space.

JUMEIRAH

🜂 SEE
Burj Al Arab 1 A3
Jumeirah Mosque.......... 2 H3
Madinat Jumeirah.......... 3 A3
Majlis Ghorfat
Um-al-Sheef.................. 4 E3

🏠 SHOP
Camel Company ....(see 3)
Fleurt...........................(see 5)
Gallery One Fine
Art Photographs...........(see 3)
Lata's ....(see 3)
Mercato Mall 5 G3
National Iranian
Carpets ....(see 3)
Persian Carpet House
& Antiques ....(see 5)
Pride of Kashmir...........(see 3)
S*uce 6 G3
Souq Madinat
Jumeirah ....(see 3)

🍽 EAT
Al Mallah 7 H3
Bella Donna ....(see 5)
Coconut Grove 8 H4
Fudo 9 F3
Maria Bonita's
Taco Shop 10 D3
Pierchic........................(see 3)
Ravi..............................11 H4
Shoo Fee Ma Fee ....(see 3)
Zheng He's...................(see 3)

🍸 DRINK
360° ....(see 1)
Agency ....(see 3)
Bahri Bar ....(see 3)
Lime Tree Café..............12 H3
Sho Cho 13 H3
Skyview Bar..................(see 1)
Ushna ....(see 3)

⭐ PLAY
Apartment....................(see 1)
Boudoir........................(see 13)
JamBase ....(see 3)
Jumeirah Beach Park ...14 E3
Kite Beach 15 C3
Madinat Theatre ....(see 3)
Open Beach 16 H3
Safa Park 17 E4
Trilogy ....(see 3)
Umm Suqeim Beach.....18 B3
Wild Wadi Waterpark....19 A3

Please see over for map

SEE

BURJ AL ARAB

☎ 301 7000; www.burj-al-arab.com;
Jumeirah Rd, Umm Suqeim

Dubai has no more fitting symbol
than the audacious Burj Al Arab
(see p23). Its dramatic white
exterior is impressive, day and
night, while its interior is simply
astonishing – and not necessarily
in a flattering way. The exterior
carries the Sydney Opera House's
sense of striking style while the
interior resembles the set from
inside the genie bottle in *I Dream
of Jeannie* TV series.

JUMEIRAH MOSQUE

☎ 353 6666 (for tour); Jumeirah Rd;
10am Thu & Sun

This splendid mosque is a sight to
behold when it is stunningly lit at
night. It can only be visited inside
on a guided tour. Put it at the top
of your 'to do' list, book ahead and
dress modestly. See p20.

Impressive Jumeirah Mosque

MADINAT JUMEIRAH

☎ 366 8888; Al-Sufouh Rd, Jumeirah
⊙ 10am-11pm

There's plenty to do at enchanting
'Jumeirah City' – explore the old
Arabian-style architecture, snoop
around splendid Al Qasr and Mina

SATWA SAUNTER

In the chaotic neighbourhood off the eat street of Al-Dhiyafah St, with its Lebanese shwarma
stands and fast-food eateries, is Satwa Rd and Satwa 'souq', a main suburban street with a
bustling souq atmosphere. The area may only be five minutes from Jumeirah Beach Rd, but
it's worlds away in many ways. A few dusty blocks from Satwa Rd, with Sheikh Zayed Rd's
swanky skyscrapers in full view, this is a poor part of town. Low-rise colourfully painted houses
have gates painted with palm trees, and chickens in the front yard. Hole-in-the-wall Afghani
bakeries sell hot bread for Dh1, and multicultural volleyball matches are held at sandy vacant
lots on Fridays. We love it.

The World
(Under Construction)

A   **B**   **C**   **D**

1

2   *Arabian
Gulf*

3

Jumeirah Rd

**UMM
SUQEIM**

Al-Sufouh Rd

Al-Wasl Rd

4

Sheikh Zayed Rd

*Interchange
No 4*
**Mall of the
Emirates;
Kempinski
Hotel**

*Interchange
No 3*

5

AL-QUOZ

6

E   F   G   H

1

2

2 km
1 mile

3

Jumeirah
Beach Park

Jumeirah Rd

JUMEIRAH

Al-Wasl Rd

Al-Satwa Rd

Iranian
Consulate

Iranian
Mosque

Satwa
Roundabout
Satwa
Post Office

Al-Dhiyafah
St

SATWA

Safa
Park

AFA

Al-Athar St

Interchange
No 2

French
Connection

Interchange
No 1

Sheikh Zayed Rd

Za'abeel
Roundabout

Muscat Rd

AL-QUOZ

ZA'ABEEL

Doha Rd

Horse
Racecourse

2nd Za'abeel Rd

5

Dubai Camel
Racecourse

AL-MARQADH

Oud Metha Rd

6

A'Salam hotels, admire the Burj Al Arab views and browse the souq. When you need to refuel there are plenty of fab waterfront restaurants and bars. Also see p21.

MAJLIS GHORFAT UM-AL-SHEEF

17 St, off Jumeirah Rd, Jumeirah; admission Dh2; ⏰ **8.30am-1.30pm & 3.30-8.30pm Sat-Thu, 3.30-8.30pm Fri**
This elegant gypsum and coral rock two-storey *majlis* (meeting place) was built in 1955 for former ruler Sheikh Rashid bin Saeed al-Maktoum to listen to his people's complaints, grievances and ideas. Beautifully restored and wonderfully decorated, it offers an authentic snapshot of Dubai during the 1950s.

SHOP

THE CAMEL COMPANY
Arts, Crafts & Souvenirs

☎ **368 6048; Souq Madinat Jumeirah, Al-Sufouh Rd;** ⏰ **10am-11pm**
Your one-stop camel-souvenir shop stocks cute camels in every conceivable texture and form – fluffy camels in Hawaiian shirts, pink camels in tutus, and plush ones so huggable you won't want to let them go – along with camel-themed notebooks, mouse pads, greeting cards, T-shirts, coffee mugs and more.

FLEURT *Fashion*

☎ **342 0906; Mercato Mall;** ⏰ **10am-10pm**
Funky, (dare we say it?) *kooky* fashion can be found on the shelves at Fleurt. When we last called in we fell in love with tailored khaki business-style jackets bearing hippy floral-patterned embroidery from Joystick, and every idiosyncratic piece by Soul Revival. Expect lots of spangles and sequins, party frocks and fun flirty fashion.

GALLERY ONE FINE ART PHOTOGRAPHS *Art*

☎ **368 6055; Souq Madinat Jumeirah, Al-Sufouh Rd;** ⏰ **10am-11pm**
These splendid framed photographs capture Dubai's traditional wind-tower architecture, Creek activity and street life. They are available in colour and black and white, and make great mementos.

LATA'S
Arts, Crafts & Souvenirs

☎ **368 6216; Souq Madinat Jumeirah, Al-Sufouh Rd;** ⏰ **10am-11pm**
Our favourite one-stop shop for Arabian and Middle Eastern souvenirs such as Moroccan lamps, brass coffee pots, antique Bedouin *khanjars* (curved daggers) and gorgeous silver prayer holders. They also have some fabulous silver jewellery, and some not-so-fabulous fake costume stuff, but

let the knowledgeable staff know your taste straight up and they won't push the tacky stuff.

🏬 MERCATO MALL
Shopping Mall

☎ 344 4161; Jumeirah Rd; ⏱ 10am-10pm Thu-Sat, 2-10pm Fri

The only things Italian about Mercato are the mall's cheesy Florentine-cum-Venetian architecture and the notable Bella Donna (p77) restaurant. You'll find the usual range of brands like Bershka, Mango and Promod; shoes, cosmetics and accessories; cinemas; and cafés well-positioned for observing the passing crowds from the light-filled courtyards.

🛍 NATIONAL IRANIAN CARPETS *Arts, Crafts & Souvenirs*

☎ 368 6003; Madinat Jumeirah, Al-Sufouh Rd; ⏱ 10am-11pm

This exceptional carpet business deals in the finest quality Iranian carpets (the best in the world) and its patient and knowledgeable staff will give you all the time in the world to ensure you find the right carpet. It's in their best interests after all. Bring photos of your home and they'll happily try to match your décor and style.

🛍 PERSIAN CARPET HOUSE & ANTIQUES *Arts, Crafts & Souvenirs*

☎ 345 6687; Mercato Mall, Jumeirah Rd; ⏱ 10am-10pm Thu-Sat, 2-10pm Fri

The outstanding Persian Carpet House stocks a wide variety of exquisite hand-woven carpets from Iran, India, Kashmir, Pakistan and Afghanistan, as well as a smaller range from Turkey, China and Russia, along with oriental antiques and curios.

🛍 PRIDE OF KASHMIR
Arts, Crafts & Souvenirs

☎ 368 6110; Madinat Jumeirah, Al-Sufouh Rd; ⏱ 10am-11pm

Specialists in Kashmiri products, this excellent store offers the best selection of genuine pashmina shawls, richly embroidered clothes and textiles. You'll also find bedspreads with beading, velvet and silk cushions, and handmade carpets from Kashmir, Afghanistan, Pakistan and Iran.

🛍 S*UCE *Fashion*

☎ 344 7270; The Village Mall, Jumeirah Rd; ⏱ 10am-10pm Sat-Thu, 4.30-10pm Fri

One of only a few truly independent boutiques in Dubai, run by three funky fashionistas, this chic store stocks idiosyncratic women's labels including Sass and Bide, Third Millennium, Tata-Naka and Tsumori Chisato. This is also the place to grab sassy accessories and jewellery, as well as very feminine home and design objects.

Shop for the perfect carpet at Souq Madinat Jumeirah

🏠 SOUQ MADINAT JUMEIRAH
Shopping Mall

☎ 366 8888; Madinat Jumeirah,
Al-Sufouh Rd, Jumeirah ⏰ 10am-11pm

While the souvenir-store prices are
higher in this re-creation of an old
Arabian souq, the quality is better
and the shopping is hassle-free.
The excellent restaurants, cafés
and bars, impressive architecture,
superb waterfront views and air-
conditioning are added incentives.
(See p21.)

🍴 EAT

🍴 **AL MALLAH** *Lebanese* $$

☎ 398 4723; Al-Dhiyafah St, Satwa;
⏰ 6am-4am

Neon-lit Al Mallah is a local favour-
ite, seeing waves of customers
converge on its outdoor terrace,
even when the thermometer is
about to burst in summer. While all
the Lebanese dishes on offer are
excellent, most people come for the
great shwarmas and fresh juices.

THE ART OF CARPET BUYING

Research, patience and persistence are of prime importance. Visit a number of carpet shops
and compare the quality and prices. Flip the corner of the rug – the more knots per square inch,
the finer the quality. Study the design – the more intricate the detail, the more expensive it
will be. Silk carpets are more valuable than wool, natural dyes more expensive than artificial.
Antique rugs are naturally dyed and appear slightly faded (this isn't a flaw). Bargain hard: feign
indecisiveness over several carpets and you'll be offered a discount for two. Even better, take
a rug-buying friend and get further discounts. Lastly, don't feel obliged to buy just because 20
carpets have been unrolled – along with the tea – this is part of the ritual. Enjoy!

🍴 BELLA DONNA *Italian* $$
☎ 344 7710; Mercato Mall, Jumeirah Rd;
🕑 11am-11pm; 🔥 Ⓥ
There's a sea change afoot at Dubai's malls, with decent food taking its place alongside the heat-lamp horrors found in chain restaurants. So we come to pay homage to Bella Donna, at the head of the mall restaurant revolution, serving up fresh pastas (the excellent Bolognese is a must) and pizzas, as well as superb coffee.

🍴 COCONUT GROVE *Goan* $$
☎ 398 3800; Rydges Plaza Hotel, Al-Dhiyafah Street, Satwa Roundabout, Satwa; 🕑 12-3pm & 7pm-12.30am
The food here is fantastic and the excellent curries (try the seafood) and biriyanis bring in regular customers who crave authentic dishes from Kerala and Goa. Reasonable prices and great views (book ahead for a window table) are a plus, but the pushy service is a major shortcoming.

🍴 FUDO *Café* $$
☎ 349 8586; off Jumeirah Beach Rd, next to Mercato Mall; 🕑 9am-3am; 🔥 Ⓥ
FUDO is a funky independent café with a delightfully eclectic interior, and a menu to match, spanning Thai, Japanese, Italian and Lebanese. Not just another standard

multicuisine eatery, this place has enough spunk to pull it off. The cool outdoor lounge is *sheesha* heaven at night.

🍴 MARIA BONITA'S TACO SHOP *Mexican* $$
☎ 395 5576; Umm al-Sheif St, Umm Suqeim; 🕑 7.30am-8pm
A welcoming little slice of Mexico (very Vera Cruz) down Jumeirah way, this laid-back eatery offers up tasty authentic dishes right down to the tortilla soup and *queso fundido* (cheese fondue). However much we wish we could order *dos cervezas* (two beers), it has no licence.

🍴 PIERCHIC *Seafood* $$$$
☎ 399 9999; Al-Qasr, Madinat Jumeirah, Al-Sufouh Rd; 🕑 noon-3pm & 7-11.30pm
The stroll down the pier to this water-bound restaurant is best taken for dinner, when Madinat Jumeirah twinkles onshore and the Burj Al Arab lightshow is mesmerising – ask for a seaside table. Slightly less mesmerising, however, is the food, so stick to the less complex dishes and enjoy the fresh seafood and romantic surrounds.

🍴 RAVI *Pakistani* $
☎ 331 5353; Al-Satwa Rd, Satwa; 🕑 24hr; 🔥 Ⓥ
Best known for its cheap prices, long opening hours and street-savvy outdoor seating, Ravi is

a Dubai institution. Stick to the vegetarian dishes, order a biriyani, and a Punjabi sweet lassi to sip on, then watch Satwa's passing parade.

🍴 SHOO FEE MA FEE
Moroccan $$$
☎ 366 8888; Souq Madinat Jumeirah, Al-Sufouh Rd; ☾ 6pm-12.30am, drinks until 2am

Literally meaning 'what's up?', what's up at Shoo Fee Ma Fee are three floors of Moroccan ambience overlooking the appealing waterways of Madinat Jumeirah. Pigeon pastilla and other Maghreb favourites offer flavour melodies as true as the authentic in-house band, but the more inventive dishes on the menu don't always hit the right notes.

🍴 ZHENG HE'S
Contemporary Chinese $$$$
☎ 366 8888; Mina A'Salam, Madinat Jumeirah, Al-Sufouh Rd; ☾ noon-3pm & 7-11.30pm

From the authentic dim sum to the inventive desserts, Zheng He's serves up wonderful flavours (try any of their seafood offerings) with eye-catching presentation. While the interior is dazzling, book well ahead for an alfresco table with a stunning view of the Burj Al Arab.

🍸 DRINK

🍸 360° *Dance Bar*
☎ 352 3500; Jumeirah Beach Hotel, Sheikh Zayed Rd; ☾ 5pm-2am

This beautiful rooftop bar with white lounges and sublime views of Burj Al Arab sees a beautiful set kicking back here on Friday evenings for sundowners, and going off when a good DJ is scheduled. Ironically, it's only doable in the cooler months when the temperatures aren't rising over 40 degrees.

🍸 THE AGENCY *Wine Bar*
☎ 366 6730; Madinat Jumeirah; ☾ noon-1am

This stylish wine bar is a good choice anytime, with comfy low leather seats for couples who want to get cosy and high tables for the groups who like to mingle. There's an excellent list of wines by the glass and tasty tapas-sized snacks – we can never get enough of the chorizo mash.

🍸 BAHRI BAR *Lounge Bar*
☎ 366 8888; Mina A' Salam, Madinat Jumeirah, Al-Sufouh Rd; ☾ noon-2am

One of Dubai's most ambient bars, Bahri is perfect for a sunset drink but save it for your last night in Dubai, because if you come on the first, we can't guarantee you won't return again, and again, and again. See also p22.

Shehab Hamad
Owner of 9714.com, Five Green, iBO

Aside from Five Green, hot places to shop for fashion and art in Dubai?
The girls at S*uce (p75) are beyond compare and The Third Line (p88) is my art spot. **Apart from iBO, best club in Dubai?** Dubai's 'interesting' speakeasies for male out-of-towners; 360° (opposite) if they're ladies. **Favourite Dubai-based fashion designer/artist/DJ?** Pink Sushi is a fun, quirky, local pop culture re-inventor; Mikey Ross is Dubai's Jeff Buckley; and Ali Ajami is our local superstar DJ/producer. **Best night to hit iBO?** Thursdays, but check 9714.com for special events. **What do you love about Dubai?** It eats its history. Often. **And dislike?** Heavy-handed censorship getting in the way of freedoms and expression. **Dubai's must-do Dubai experiences?** Dubai Museum, an *abra* (water taxi) ride across Dubai Creek.

NEIGHBOURHOODS

JUMEIRAH

🍸 LIME TREE CAFÉ *Café*
☎ 349 8498; Near Jumeirah Mosque,
Jumeirah Rd; ⏱ 7.30am-8pm; 👶
Second home to Dubai's *Stepford
Wives* on weekdays, this bright
green villa (head for the terrace)
is in a state of perpetual 'coffee
morning'. Although the coffee
is excellent, the service could be
better. Still, it is a fascinating expat
institution-cum-'expat-in-a-bub-
ble'-sociological experiment.

Breathtaking vistas from Skyview Bar at Burj Al Arab

SHO CHO *Dance Bar*
☎ 346 1111; Dubai Marine Beach Resort & Spa, Jumeirah Rd; ⏰ 7pm-1am Sat-Wed, 7pm-2am Thu & Fri

During the hot summer months chill out to the DJ's vibes while lounging on the funky white leather sofas in this groovy sushi bar. In winter the DJ moves outside to the wooden beachside deck so Dubai's hipsters can take in the balmy breeze, deep house and tribal beats, and each other.

SKYVIEW BAR *Cocktail Bar*
☎ 301 7777; Burj Al Arab, Jumeirah Rd; ⏰ 11am-2am

It may be cocktail bar of the world's first seven-star hotel, but a window seat could be required to divert your attention from the lurid décor to the dizzying coastal views. Phone ahead, booking with credit card required. Have one drink to say you've done it then think about moving on to Bahri Bar (p22).

USHNA *Lounge Bar*
☎ 368 6506; Souq Madinat Jumeirah, Al-Sufouh Rd; ⏰ 6pm-2am

The Indian fusion restaurant may be glam (fuchsia interior, hanging seats and chandeliers) but the funky candle-lit bar outside is sub-lime. Settle into a lounge, listen to some chilled vibes, and savour the Madinat Jumeirah views and buzzy crowd below on weekends.

PLAY

THE APARTMENT
Lounge Bar
☎ 406 8000; Jumeirah Beach Hotel; ⏰ 8pm-3am

Chilling out in a leather armchair in the deluxe lounge of this rather exclusive club might have you thinking you're at a party at someone's very chic apartment, perhaps until you hit the club where some of the hottest DJs entice clubbers onto the dance floor.

BOUDOIR *Dance Club*
☎ 345 5995; Dubai Marine Beach Resort, Jumeirah Rd; ⏰ 7.30pm-3am

Red velvet booths, hanging glass beads and crystal chandeliers make baroque Boudoir one of Dubai's most glamorous bars. Starting the night in style as a restaurant-cum-cocktail bar, it becomes a decadent dance club when the clock strikes 12.

JAMBASE *Live Music*
☎ 366 6550; Souq Madinat Jumeirah, Al-Sufouh Rd; ⏰ 7pm-2am

This stylish venue is the place to head for live jazz, R&B and soul, as well as fresh fusion cuisine (it also offers a pre-theatre menu). The bands know how to work a crowd and the dance floor jumps on weekends.

⭐ JUMEIRAH BEACH PARK
Beach Park

☎ 349 2555; Jumeirah Rd; per person/ car Dh5/20; ⏱ 8am-10.30pm, women & children only Sat

With its shady palm trees, manicured lawns and long stretch of beach, Dubai's favourite park gets packed on weekends. Facilities are excellent, with a children's playground, barbeques, picnic tables and kiosks, as well as lifeguards on duty.

⭐ KITE BEACH *Beach*
Umm Suqeim 4

There's plenty of room to sunbathe comfortably on this long pristine beach while you watch the action provided by the local kite surfer community (hence the name), whose abilities range from good to good grief. No facilities.

⭐ MADINAT THEATRE *Theatre*
☎ 366 6546, 366 6550; Souq Madinat Jumeirah, Al-Sufouh Rd, Jumeirah; tickets Dh60-200; ⏱ box office 10am-11pm, show times vary

Soak up the sun at Jumeirah Beach

A regular programme of crowd-pleasing entertainment from the Russian State Ballet to Broadway musicals keeps Dubai's culture-starved residents happy. Performances may take place in the gorgeous theatre, the big arena, or outdoors at the enchanting waterside amphitheatre.

☆ OPEN BEACH *Beach*
Next to Dubai Marin Beach Resort & Spa
Also known as Russian Beach, because of its popularity with Russian tourists, this stretch of white sand gets crowded with a mix of sun-worshippers and expats from the 'hood. On Fridays guest workers also like to hang out here on their day off. There are showers and a kiosk.

☆ SAFA PARK *Park*
☎ 349 2111; cnr Al-Wasl Rd & Al-Hadiqa St, Safa; admission Dh5; ⏱ 8am-11pm, women & children only Tue
Popular with Jumeirah families, the facilities at this verdant park keep everyone happy. There are tennis courts, a soccer pitch, barbecues, a lake with paddleboats, and even an artificial waterfall.

☆ TRILOGY *Dance Club*
☎ 366 6917; Souq Madinat Jumeirah, Al-Sufouh Rd; ⏱ 9pm-3am
Dubai's hottest dance club, arabesque-styled Trilogy has

dance floors and bars catering to different tastes over several levels, and an impressive programme of international DJs. To avoid the queues get there early and head to the Rooftop Bar for drinks, or buy tickets in advance.

☆ UMM SUQEIM BEACH *Beach*
Next to Jumeirah Beach Hotel, Jumeirah Beach Rd
Between Jumeirah Beach Hotel and Kite Beach, this white sand beach with fabulous views of the Burj Al Arab is popular with Jumeirah families and a more body-conscious set as well as surfers during the winter months. There are showers but little shelter, so don't forget that sunscreen.

☆ WILD WADI WATERPARK *Water Park*
☎ 348 4444; www.wildwadi.com; Jumeirah Rd; adult/child (under 13) Dh140/120; ⏱ 11am-6pm Nov-Feb, 11am-7pm Mar-May & Sep-Oct, 11am-9pm June-Aug
There's no better way to cool down in Dubai than heading to Wild Wadi for the day. This popular water park caters for everyone with sedate rides for young kids and nervous adults, and two Flowriders (artificial waves) and the terrifying Jumeirah Sceirah for the more adventurous. Hint: keep your legs closed and hang on to your swimmers.

> SHEIKH ZAYED RD

Dubai's residents speed down Sheikh Zayed Rd but visitors to the city should turn off and head into a hotel with a view to take in the striking architecture on this sleek strip. A number of attention-grabbing edifices having opened here in the last few years making the strip seem like a host to some kind of freeform architectural jazz, where each new development riffs off the last. Check out the eye-catching Dusit Dubai and World Trade Centre. Just a few blocks from the road are several sights that couldn't be more different from each other. To appreciate these varied themes, check out Nad al-Sheba Racing Club and Camel Racecourse, the pretty prink flamingos at Ras Al-Khor Wildlife Sanctuary and the art galleries of industrial Al-Quoz.

SHEIKH ZAYED RD

SEE
Art Space 1 H3
B21 Gallery 2 B3
Dubai Camel
Racecourse 3 F5
Godolphin Gallery ......(see 14)
Ras Al-Khor Wildlife
Sanctuary 4 H5
Third Line 5 B3
Total Arts at the
Courtyard 6 C3

SHOP
Aizone ....(see 8)
Al Jaber Gallery ....(see 8)
Azza Fahmy Jewellery..(see 7)
Camper ....(see 8)
Charles & Keith ....(see 8)
Emilio Pucci ....(see 7)
Forever 21 ....(see 8)

Harvey Nichols ....(see 8)
Jimmy Choo...................(see 7)
Jumeirah Emirates Towers
Shopping Boulevard 7 H3
Mall of the Emirates......8 A3
Pixi.................................(see 8)
Rectangle Jaune............(see 8)
Villa Moda ....(see 7)
Virgin Megastore ....(see 8)

EAT
Almaz by Momo ....(see 8)
Benjarong......................9 G3
Emporio Armani Caffé .(see 8)
Exchange Grill ....(see 1)
Noodle House ....(see 12)
Olive House 10 G3
Sezzam..........................(see 8)
Spectrum on One ....(see 1)
Trader Vic's..................11 H3
Vu's...............................12 H3

DRINK
1897 Bar ....(see 8)
Agency ....(see 7)
Après ....(see 8)
Cin Cin's ....(see 1)
Lotus One 13 H3
Vu's Bar........................(see 12)

PLAY
Dubai Community
Theatre & Arts Centre
(DUCTAC) ....(see 8)
Nad al-Sheba
Racing Club 14 F6
Peppermint Club ....(see 1)
Ski Dubai ....(see 8)
Softtouch Spa ....(see 8)
Zinc...............................(see 11)

Please see over for map

SEE

ART SPACE

☎ 332 5523; www.artspace-dubai.com;
The Fairmont Hotel, Sheikh Zayed Rd;
🕑 10am-8.30pm Sat-Thu

This contemporary gallery dedicated to promoting national and international work and nurturing the local scene has exhibited pop art by Emirati Mohamed Kanoo and powerful work by Iranian female artists, such as Shadafarin Ghadarian. There are new exhibitions each month.

B21 GALLERY

☎ 340 3965; www.b21gallery.com; near The Courtyard and Third Line, off Sheikh Zayed Rd, between Interchanges 3 & 4, Al-Quoz; 🕑 10am-2pm Sat-Thu, 5-8pm Fri

Palestinian artist Jeffar Khaldi shows his own vibrant art, as well as rotating exhibitions of locally produced and regional work, such as Shadi Ghadirian's thought-provoking portraits. Worth calling in if you're in this developing arts neighbourhood, but if you're not, call first, as they could be in the middle of hanging an exhibition.

New visual directions at Art Space

A **B** **C** **D**

1

2

Jumeirah Rd

UMM
SUQEIM

94

Al-Wasl Rd

92

SAFA

65

Sheikh Zayed Rd

3
*Interchange
No 4*

*Interchange
No 3*

11

5 6

2

*Mall of
the Emirates;
Kempinski Hotel*

AL-QUOZ

4

63

5

6

0   2 km

0   1 mile

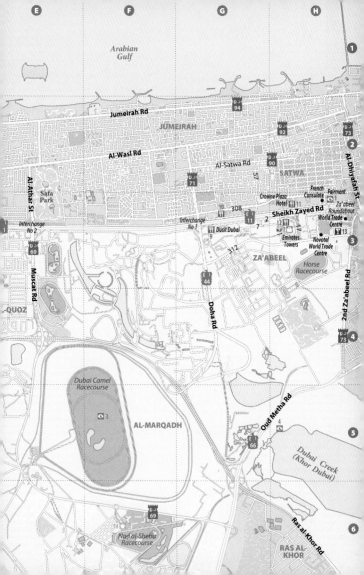

☪ DUBAI CAMEL RACECOURSE

☎ 338 2324; off Oud Metha Rd near Nad al-Sheba Club

Camel racing is a major spectator sport in the UAE, with races starting at around 7am and continuing until about 9am on weekends. If you miss the races, snap the more photogenic camel walks from their farms across to the track to train. Best time is 5pm. (Also see p26).

☪ GODOLPHIN GALLERY

☎ 336 3666; www.nadalshebaclub .com; Nad al-Sheba, off Sheikh Zayed Rd, Interchange 2, Al-Marqadh; adult/child Dh170/80; ⏰ 7-11am Mon, Wed & Sat, Sep-Jun

Visited as part of a tour of Nad al-Sheba racecourse, this excellent museum is packed with photographs, trophies, horseracing paraphernalia and interactive displays charting the extraordinary success of the Godolphin stables. It's a must for racing fans. Book in advance.

☪ RAS AL-KHOR WILDLIFE SANCTUARY

☎ 338 2324; off Oud Metha Rd, on the way to Nad al-Sheba Horse Racing Club; admission free; ⏰ 9am-4pm Sat-Thu

Spy on Dubai's 3000-plus pink flamingo population, which flocks here during the winter months, from excellent viewing hides. Powerful binoculars can be borrowed to get a close-up of the birds without disturbing them. The juxtaposition of these elegant birds against the Dubai metropolis is amazing. Also known somewhat confusingly as Al-Khor Nature Reserve and the Dubai Creek Waterbird and Wildlife Sanctuary.

☪ THE THIRD LINE

☎ 394 3194; www.thethirdline.com; next to The Courtyard, off Sheikh Zayed Rd, Interchange 3, Al-Quoz; ⏰ 11am-8pm Sat-Thu

Talented young curators Sunny Rahbar (see opposite) and Claudia Cellini operate Dubai's most adventurous art space. Consistently impressive exhibitions of contemporary Middle Eastern art have shown provocative work that often breaks the rules to create refreshing new forms. Sign up to their mailing list so you don't miss out on the glam champagne openings.

☪ TOTAL ARTS AT THE COURTYARD

☎ 228 2888; www.courtyard-uae.com; The Courtyard, off Sheikh Zayed Rd, Interchange 3, Al-Quoz; ⏰ 10am-1pm & 4-8pm Sat-Thu

In a modern courtyard complex with artists' workshops, designers, craftsmen and media companies, Total Arts holds changing exhibitions of contemporary art and Islamic calligraphy, along with rare

Sunny Rahbar
Co-Owner & Director, The Third Line (opposite)

What do you love about Dubai? I grew up here and I love that there are people from all over the world living here working together. **Why should people visit?** Dubai makes people see the Middle East in a different light. **What's inspiring about Dubai for artists?** The changes taking place; watching that and being part of that can inspire artists to respond through their work. **Favourite artists?** Raghda Bukhash, Amna al Zaabi and Lamya Gargash: all young Emirati women with a lot to say. Their work is identity-based, so it's interesting to see how they respond to changes. **Aside from The Third Line, best place to see/buy art?** Art Space (p85), B21 (p85), Total Arts at the Courtyard (opposite), XVA (p59). **Tips for art-lovers?** Visit Sharjah Museum (p45) and time your trip to coincide with Sharjah Biennial or Gulf Art Fair. **Your personal favourites?** Brunch at More (p49), dinner at Maya (p106), drinks at The Agency (p78).

NEIGHBOURHOODS

SHEIKH ZAYED RD

carpets, textiles and sculptures by local and regional artists. Also check out The Courtyard Gallery while you're here.

SHOP

AIZONE *Fashion*

☎ 347 9333; Mall of the Emirates, Sheikh Zayed Rd; ⏱ 10am-10pm Sun-Wed, 10am-midnight Thu-Sat

You can lose yourself for hours in this enormous Lebanese fashion emporium. Room after room hangs with hip, hard-to-find fashion from American Retro, Plenty, Bibelot, Citizens of Humanity, Lotus and Da-Nang, plus many more. A fashionista's idea of heaven.

AL JABER GALLERY
Arts, Crafts & Souvenirs

☎ 341 4103; Mall of the Emirates, Sheikh Zayed Rd; ⏱ 10am-10pm Sun-Wed, 10am-midnight Thu-Sat

This is an offshoot of the City Centre store, offering an even wider selection of Oriental and Arabian handicrafts, souvenirs and carpets from the Middle East and India, from brass coffee-pots to Bedouin *khanjars* (curved daggers).

AZZA FAHMY JEWELLERY
Jewellery

☎ 330 0340; Emirates Towers Shopping Boulevard, Sheikh Zayed Rd; ⏱ 10am-10pm Sat-Thu, 4-10pm Fri

Azza Fahmy Jewellery displays exquisite creations

Egyptian Azza Fahmy's coveted jewellery draws on Islamic and Arab traditions, combining classical Arabic poetry and Islamic wisdom in fine calligraphy with gemstones, beads and motifs; and elements from different ages and civilisations. Souvenirs don't come more precious than this.

CAMPER *Fashion*
☎ 340 9789; Mall of the Emirates, Sheikh Zayed Rd; ◷ 10am-10pm Sun-Wed, 10am-midnight Thu-Sat

The opening of Dubai's first Camper store meant local hipsters no longer had to travel all the way to Barcelona for these funky, functional leather shoes and sneakers – crafted with centuries-old shoe-making techniques – although it was a good excuse while it lasted.

CHARLES & KEITH *Fashion*
☎ 341 0408; Mall of the Emirates, Sheikh Zayed Rd; ◷ 10am-10pm Sun-Wed, 10am-midnight Thu-Sat

Singaporeans Charles and Keith Wong produce sassy feminine, affordable shoes with fab attention to detail – pretty clogs with big cotton bows, strappy sandals with beading, slingbacks with buckles. The summery, open styles are perfect for Dubai's year-round sunshine and stifling heat.

EMILIO PUCCI *Fashion*
☎ 330 0660; Blvd at Emirates Towers, Sheikh Zayed Rd; ◷ 10am-10pm Sat-Thu, 4-10pm Fri

Dubai's first and only Pucci store is worth visiting just to check out the groovy interior, but you'll also find a colourful and funky range of psychedelic fashion, accessories and handbags – more affordable here than anywhere.

FOREVER 21 *Fashion*
☎ 341 3412; Mall of the Emirates, Sheikh Zayed Rd; ◷ 10am-10pm Sun-Wed, 10am-midnight Thu-Sat

One of only four stores in this part of the globe belonging to this mega-North American H&M-style franchise, this one is Dubai's largest with the biggest range of fun, youthful, affordable, disposable fashion and accessories – so cheap, you'll leave the store laden with shopping bags.

HARVEY NICHOLS *Department Store*
☎ 341 3833; Mall of the Emirates, Sheikh Zayed Rd; ◷ 10am-10pm Sun-Wed, 10am-midnight Thu-Sat

The cool, contemporary design of newcomer Harvey Nic's – the largest outside the UK – and its discerning fashion collections are already drawing Dubai's fashionistas here in droves. The store's signature offerings – from a Personal Shopping

Suite to exclusive concierge service Quintessentially – suit Dubai's VIP-loving shoppers to a tee.

☐ JIMMY CHOO *Footwear*
☎ 330 0404; Emirates Towers Shopping Boulevard, Sheikh Zayed Rd; ⌚ 10am-10pm Sat-Thu, 4-10pm Fri

The shoes that found fame on the feet of sexy sitcom stars are now a household name in Dubai. Recline on the chaise longue at the fabulous flagship store so you can see the miracles these heavenly creatures work.

☐ JUMEIRAH EMIRATES TOWERS SHOPPING BOUVELARD *Shopping Mall*
☎ 330 0000; Jumeirah Emirates Towers, Sheikh Zayed Rd; ⌚ 10am-10pm Sat-Thu, 4-10pm Fri

This exclusive shopping arcade in Emirates Towers is home to swish designer boutiques such as Armani and Gucci on the ground level and Pucci and Jimmy Choo upstairs, along with our favourite, chic Villa Moda. Noodle House (p94) is here when you need to refuel, and The Agency (p96) for shopping post mortems.

☐ MALL OF THE EMIRATES *Shopping Mall*
☎ 409 9000; www.malloftheemirates .com; Sheikh Zayed Rd; ⌚ 10am-10pm Sun-Wed, 10am-midnight Thu-Sat

This opulent mall is one of Dubai's best and busiest. Their excellent website has a day planner allowing you to create your personal mall itinerary so you can maximise your shopping time. Along with the usual franchises, there's Harvey Nichols and some excellent eateries.

☐ PIXI *Cosmetics*
☎ 347 3833; Mall of the Emirates, Sheikh Zayed Rd; ⌚ 10am-10pm Sun-Wed, 10am-midnight Thu-Sat

This fabulous cosmetics brand was the brainchild of three Swedish make-up artist sisters, Petra, Sara and Sofia, who began creating their own fantastic products out of a sense of frustration of not being able to find what they wanted. Their 'awakening eye beauty kit' works wonders after a late night on Dubai's dance floors.

☐ RECTANGLE JAUNE *Fashion*
☎ 341 0288; Mall of the Emirates, Sheikh Zayed Rd; ⌚ 10am-10pm Sun-Wed, 10am-midnight Thu-Sat

Lebanese guys have a real sense of style, and it's no wonder when Lebanon has so many chic male fashion labels. Rectangle Jaune is one of the smartest, specialising in well-cut shirts, trousers, suits and ties in bold colours and textures that work surprisingly well together even when they shouldn't. This is the only store outside of Lebanon.

 VILLA MODA *Fashion*

☎ 330 4555; Emirates Towers Shopping Boulevard, Sheikh Zayed Rd; ⏱ 10am-10pm Sat-Thu, 4-10pm Fri

The sexy *2001: A Space Odyssey* interior is reason enough to visit Kuwait 'Sheikh of Chic' Majed al-Sabah's one-stop-designer-shop. It's an added bonus that its curvy capsulelike boutiques are home to the hottest fashion, including Alexander McQueen, Easton Pearson, Stella McCartney and Marni.

VIRGIN MEGASTORE
Music & DVDs

☎ 341 4353; Mall of the Emirates, Sheikh Zayed Rd; ⏱ 10am-10pm Sun-Wed, 10am-midnight Thu-Sat

Virgin's newest store in Dubai is massive, offering an enormous selection of musical souvenirs from the Middle East, such as traditional Oud and Oriental-infused House. There's also an excellent selection of DVDs and books from the region and a great range of Apple products and iPods.

🍽 EAT

🍽 ALMAZ BY MOMO
Moroccan $$

☎ 409 8877; Mall of the Emirates; ⏱ 10am-midnight Sun-Thu, 10am-1.30am Fri, 10am-midnight Sat; Ⓥ

Restaurateur Mourad 'Momo' Mazouz, creator of Sketch and Momo

Almaz by Momo for chic dining

in London, has made what many consider an odd move by opening up in a mall in Dubai. The diverse space is a stunning success, offering a groovy *sheesha* room, a stylish salon for snacks and (non-alcoholic) drinks, a sophisticated restaurant serving up Maghreb classics, a Moroccan patisserie and funky boutique.

🍽 BENJARONG *Thai* $$$$

☎ 343 3333; Dusit Dubai; ⏱ 7.30pm-midnight; Ⓥ

Refinement is the key word at this elegant Royal Thai restaurant, from the discreet traditional Thai music and dance to the attentive service. However, there's nothing understated about the fantastic flavours, with soups such as the *tom yam goong* packing a pungent punch, and the mains are equally flavourful. If you like it hot, tell them.

EMPORIO ARMANI CAFFÉ *Italian* $$

☎ 341 0591; Mall of the Emirates; 10am-11.30pm Sat-Thu, 2pm-midnight Fri; V

The revolution in Dubai's mall food offers no better example than this outpost of the Armani empire. The coffee is as smooth as an Italian waiter, the food is as stylishly presented as the staff, and the Italian flavours are so good we wish they had a liquor licence.

EXCHANGE GRILL *Steakhouse* $$$$

☎ 311 8000; The Fairmont Hotel; 7pm-midnight

This is the most elegant of Dubai's numerous steakhouses after its recent makeover. The hushed ambience allows you to fully concentrate on the menu featuring prime cuts of meat and well-chosen vintage wines. A meat-lover's paradise.

NOODLE HOUSE *Asian* $$

☎ 319 8757; Emirates Towers; noon-11.30pm; V

Given the success of the Noodle House, we've been half expecting the standards to drop, however, the pan-Asian staples here (try the char *kway teow* or the laksa) are always fresh and it's only those communal tables (sometimes impossible to get comfortable at) that stop us eating here every day.

OLIVE HOUSE *Lebanese/Mediterranean* $$

☎ 343 3110; Tower One; 9am-midnight; V

While this stylish little place has a bit of an identity crisis (is it a bakery, Lebanese restaurant, delicatessen or pizza place?), the food's uniformly good – as is the coffee. The pizzas are fresh, wonderful wood-fired numbers and the *manaeesh* (Middle Eastern dough topped with cheese or *zaatar* or ground meat) are the tastiest around.

SEZZAM *Global* $$

☎ 341 0000; Kempinski Mall of the Emirates; 11.30am-11.30pm; V

This restaurant is so huge it almost surpasses the sight of skiers and snowboarders heading down the slopes of the adjacent Ski Dubai (p98). With global cuisine labelled under the Flame, Bake or Steam monikers, it's really a food court with style – and a great place for a break when on a shopping excursion at this massive mall.

SPECTRUM ON ONE
Modern Global $$$
☎ 311 8101; The Fairmont Hotel;
🕑 7pm-1am; 👶 Ⓥ

Eight open kitchens serving up cuisine from around the globe may sound more food court than

NEIGHBOURHOODS

SHEIKH ZAYED RD

Spectrum on One plates up versatile cuisine

five star, but Spectrum on One is one of Dubai's most consistently good restaurants. While it's still an odd sight to see one diner gobbling down fresh oysters while a companion tackles a green curry, the ability to sate disparate tastes with aplomb is this restaurant's forte.

🍴 TRADER VIC'S
Polynesian $$$$
☎ 331 1111; Crowne Plaza Hotel;
🕑 12.30-3pm & 7.30-11.30pm
This branch of the Polynesian-themed chain has been here longer than the pyramids. We love it for its lethal Mai Tai cocktails, excellent starter plates to share, and brilliant filet mignon and Peking duck pancakes. We'll not apologise for it being a bit of a guilty pleasure, with its cheesy décor and only-good-when-you're-drunk house band. Please enjoy.

🍴 VU'S *Fine Dining* $$$$
☎ 319 8771; Emirates Towers;
🕑 12.30-3pm & 7.30-11.30pm
While this restaurant atop Emirates Tower has been a bit of a high stakes gamble in the past (unless you're dining on someone else's expense account), with a new Australian chef at the helm it has fast become one of Dubai's more consistent fine-dining ex-

periences. It already had the wow factor in spades – a chic interior and spectacular views – and now it has impressive cuisine to match.

🍸 DRINK

🍸 1897 BAR *Cocktail Bar*
☎ 341 0000; Mall of the Emirates, Sheikh Zayed Rd; 🕑 noon-1am
Few bars are more alluring than 1897, with its lounge soundtrack, flickering candles, arabesque-patterned walls, and chic purple velvet bar stools and low sofas. But while the atmosphere is seductive enough, the cocktails by expert mixologist Sasha (formerly of Trilogy) are positively addictive – try the delicious purple Brumble (Bombay Sapphire and Chambord). The regulars are as beautiful as the bar.

🍸 THE AGENCY *Wine Bar*
☎ 330 0000; Emirates Towers Shopping Boulevard, Sheikh Zayed Rd; 🕑 noon-1am Sat-Thu, 3pm-1am Fri
An extensive wine list, excellent vintages by the glass, themed tasting selections, and delicious tapas-sized snacks keep this stylish wine bar busy, particularly on week nights when it gets popular with the besuited Emirates Towers' set.

APRÈS *Lounge Bar*

☎ 341 2575; Mall of the Emirates, Sheikh Zayed Rd; ⏲ noon-2am

This funky low-key bar is Dubai's first in a mall (how they swung *that* remains a mystery), making it perfect for post-movie or shopping spree post mortems. Adjacent to Ski Dubai, with fabulous snowy vistas, it's also an ideal après ski/snowboarding bar (obviously the idea). While it does excellent cocktails, looking out at the snow always makes us feel like looking for mulled wine.

CIN CIN'S *DJ Bar*

☎ 311 8316; The Fairmont Hotel, Sheikh Zayed Rd; ⏲ 6pm-2am

This chic spot with stunningly lit bar and colour-changing ice buckets (yes, that's right) has Dubai's finest wines-by-the-glass lists and best bar food. While the freshly shucked oysters are tempting we can never resist the divine Wagyu Beef Burger flight, assorted tiny-sized burgers served with rosemary and sea-salted fries. Check it out on Tuesday and Thursday champagne nights when DJ Stickyfingers spins some smooth sounds.

LOTUS ONE *DJ Bar*

☎ 329 3200; World Trade Centre, off Sheikh Zayed Rd; ⏲ noon-2am

While the colour-shifting fibre-optic lighting, swinging seats and sand under the glass floor make this one of Dubai's most stylish-looking bars, its Asian-inspired bar snacks and cocktails are excellent. It's at its best when there's a good DJ on.

VU'S BAR *Champagne Bar*

☎ 330 0000; 51st fl, Emirates Towers, Sheikh Zayed Rd; ⏲ 6pm-2am

The stupendous views of Dubai draw the tourists up the glass elevator, but residents come for the decent wines by the glass, stylish setting and buzzy atmosphere.

COMEDY CENTRAL

Once so starved of culture and interesting entertainment, Dubai has seen a spate of interesting performers visiting the city, especially comedians, from American post-punk performance poet Henry Rollins (at DUCTAC; see p113) to Arab-American comedian Ahmed Ahmed (for a one-off gig at the Radisson SAS Dubai Media City; see p113).

For a city in a region that's often criticised for its censorship, it was interesting to see both guys doing politically-charged skits focused on politics and racism. Ahmed Ahmed in particular rocked the room with his tales of being Arab-American in the US since 9/11.

Check *What's On* and *Time Out* magazines to see whose performing when you're in town.

PLAY

⭐ DUBAI COMMUNITY THEATRE AND ARTS CENTRE (DUCTAC) *Theatre*

☎ 341 4777; www.ductac.org; level 2, Mall of the Emirates; 🕑 9am-10pm Sat-Thu, 11am-10pm Fri

Filling a much-needed void in Dubai's cultural scene, DUCTAC hosts classical music, opera, drama and musicals, and art exhibitions, along with art workshops.

⭐ NAD AL SHEBA RACING CLUB *Racecourse*

☎ 336 3666; www.dubairacingclub .com; Nad al-Sheba District 5km south-east of Dubai centre

While Dubai's racing season starts in November, the Dubai International Racing Carnival, held from late January through to the end of March, is when things really hot up. It culminates in the Dubai World Cup (www.dubaiworldcup .com), the world's richest horse race, with prize money of a dizzying US$6 million and a total purse for the event of over US$20 million.

⭐ PEPPERMINT CLUB *Dance Club*

☎ 332 0037; www.peppermint-club .com; The Fairmont Hotel, Sheikh Zayed Rd; 🕑 10pm-3am Fri

Glam Peppermint takes over the Fairmont's Barajeel Ballroom to host Dubai's biggest weekly club night, attracting devoted regulars who wouldn't dance anywhere else on a Friday. If travelling, check its site to see where else you can taste the Peppermint Experience – last time we checked they were taking the Dubai night to Moscow.

⭐ SKI DUBAI *Indoor Ski Resort*

☎ 409 4000; www.skidxb.com; Mall of the Emirates, Sheikh Zayed Rd; Snowpark Dh60, Ski slope (2 hr) adult/child Dh150/130; 🕑 10am-11pm Sun-Wed, 10am-midnight Thu-Sat

Dubai's first indoor ski resort (yes, there's *another* coming) has all bases covered; a kids' snowpark, a gentle beginners' slope and the world's first indoor black run for those who like it steep. A quad lift takes skiers and boarders up to two stations and there's a magic carpet for beginners. The snow uses no chemicals – it's 'real' snow that falls overnight at around -10 degrees Celcius. Just bring gloves – all equipment is incorporated in the price, including disposable socks.

⭐ SOFTTOUCH SPA *Spa*

☎ 341 0000; Kempinski Mall of the Emirates Hotel, Sheikh Zayed Rd; 🕑 9am-10pm

One of Dubai's newest spas, the Softtouch Spa has quickly

Crowd-pleasing beats pump out at Zinc

become one of its best, with its tranquil Asian-minimalist interiors – slate floors, Thai silk walls and orange hanging lamps – Ayurvedic treatments, expert staff and beautiful Ligne St Barth products.

⭐ **ZINC** *Dance Club*
☎ 331 1111; Crowne Plaza Hotel, Sheikh Zayed Rd; ⏰ 7pm-3am
After a sexy 2006 makeover, Zinc remains popular with a mixed crowd of expats and tourists who like to party, hitting the dance floor early in the night compared to most Dubai clubs.

> NEW DUBAI

When the newer developments of Dubai Marina and its city of skyscrapers seemingly appeared out of nowhere, and new residential developments started to line Sheikh Zayed Rd from Interchange 5 onwards toward Jebel Ali – an area that had just been desert a few years ago – Dubai residents and the city's media started to call these areas New Dubai and the name stuck. The area is really just an extension of Jumeirah, filling a gap that previously existed between the last of the Jumeirah Beach hotels and Jebel Ali, but with its sleek high-rise apartments and luxury yachts, and the international nouveau riche that are buying them up, New Dubai feels very different from old Jumeirah with its low-rise white villas and bougainvillea-filled gardens. Not to mention the antithesis of old Dubai, down by the Creek.

NEW DUBAI

🛍 SHOP

Bauhaus	(see 1)
Ginger & Lace	(see 1)
Ibn Batutta Mall	1 B4
Mumbai Sei	(see 1)
Paris Gallery	(see 1)

🍴 EAT

Bice	2 D3
Certo	3 F4
Chandelier	(see 5)
Eauzone	4 E3
Indego	5 E4

Maya	6 E3
Nina	(see 4)
Tagine	(see 4)
Tang	7 E3

🍸 DRINK

Bar 44	(see 5)
Barasti Bar	(see 7)
Buddha Bar	(see 5)
Maya	(see 7)
Media Lounge	(see 3)
Rooftop	(see 4)
Tamanya Terrace	(see 3)

⭐ PLAY

Emirates Golf Club	8 E4
Oriental Hammam	(see 4)
Sheesha Courtyard	(see 4)

Please see over for map

SHOP

BAUHAUS *Fashion*

☎ 368 5551; Ibn Battuta Mall, Sheikh Zayed Rd; ✆ 10am-10pm Sat-Tue, 10am-midnight Wed-Fri

Dubai's hipsters make it a habit to drop into Bauhaus frequently for its edgy fashion – from Evisu jeans to Philipp Plein and Antik Denim – street art, interesting CDs and occasional parties featuring live DJs, catwalk shows and graffiti art.

GINGER & LACE *Fashion*

☎ 368 5109; Ibn Battuta Mall, Sheikh Zayed Rd; ✆ 10am-10pm Sat-Tue, 10am-midnight Wed-Fri

Owner Sahar Yassin-Mekkawi started Ginger & Lace so she wouldn't have to travel overseas to buy funky fashion. She offers up an eclectic selection of colourful, whimsical fashion, reflecting her own idiosyncratic taste, including high-spirited labels Anna Sui, Betsey Johnson, Ingwa, Melero, Tibi, Ananya, Sass and Bide, and Wheels and Doll Baby.

IBN BATTUTA MALL *Shopping Mall*

☎ 362 1900; Sheikh Zayed Rd; ✆ 10am-10pm Sat-Tue, 10am-midnight Wed-Fri

Fourteenth-century Arab scholar Ibn Battuta travelled 75,000 miles from China to Andalusia over 30 years, and you'll appreciate how

Ginger & Lace brings innovative fashion labels to Ibn Battuta Mall

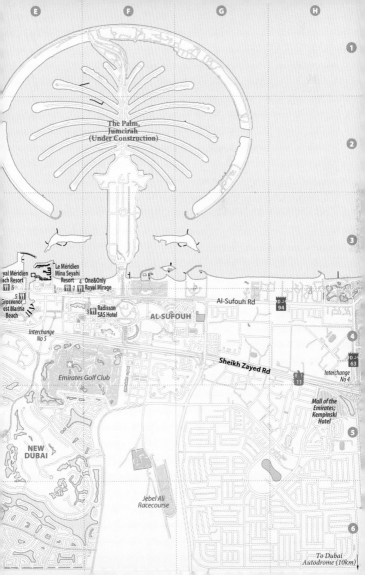

E **F** **G** **H**

1

The Palm,
Jumeirah
(Under Construction)

2

3

al Méridien
ach Resort
6

Le Méridien
Mina Seyahi
Resort

5
Grosvenor
est Marina
Beach

One&Only
Royal Mirage

Radisson
SAS Hotel

AL-SUFOUH

Al-Sufouh Rd

94

4

Interchange
No 5

Sheikh Zayed Rd

E
11

63

Interchange
No 4

Emirates Golf Club

Mall of the
Emirates;
Kempinski
Hotel

5

NEW
DUBAI

Jebel Ali
Racecourse

6

To Dubai
Autodrome (10km)

tired he must have been after trekking through this mall. Kids can do storytelling tours and a virtual magic carpet ride across Dubai and take a tape home to prove it. There's also some great shopping.

MUMBAI SEI
Fashion & Homewares
☎ 366 9855; India Court, Ibn Battuta Mall, Sheikh Zayed Rd; ⏱ 10am-10pm Sat-Tue, 10am-midnight Wed-Fri
This exotic fashion and interiors emporium stocks coveted Indian labels that combine contemporary elements with traditional Indian styles. Our favourites are the fabulous Ranna caftans with gorgeous embroidery and gems, Renu Tandon's extravagant Mejnah label, and Meera Mahadevia's tiny handcrafted bags embellished with semiprecious stones and fringing.

PARIS GALLERY *Cosmetics*
☎ 368 5500; Ibn Battuta Mall, Sheikh Zayed Rd; ⏱ 10am-10pm Sat-Tue, 10am-midnight Wed-Fri
The best branch of the UAE's most popular beauty chain stocks a huge range of international perfumes and cosmetics, handbags and accessories. There's also a Comfort Zone spa, a Perfume Cocktail Bar where you can have your own perfumes mixed, and a chocolate, coffee shop and juice bar. Sales staff can be pushy but

they do give discounts and have regular promotions where extra treats are dropped into your bag.

EAT

BICE *Italian* $$$$
☎ 399 1111; Hilton Dubai Jumeirah, Al-Sufouh Rd, Al-Mina al-Seyahi; ⏱ noon-3pm & 7pm-midnight; Ⅴ
The godfather of Italian cuisine in Dubai, this understated, elegant restaurant uses quality imported ingredients and treats them with respect – all too rare a combination in this city. Excellent breads, a well-selected wine list and well-drilled staff help cement its reputation.

CERTO *Italian* $$$
☎ 366 9111; Radisson SAS Hotel, Dubai Media City; ⏱ noon-3.30pm & 7pm-midnight; Ⅴ
One of the best new restaurant openings in Dubai, Certo delivers fresh Italian fare in a stunning space dominated by a 6m-high 'wine tower'. Everything from pizza to pasta (try the parpadelle with duck and broccoli) to risotto is made fresh, overseen by an Italian chef – something all too rare in Dubai's Italian eateries.

CHANDELIER *Lebanese* $$$
☎ 366 3606; Marina Walk, Dubai Marina, Al-Sufouh Rd, Al-Mina al-Seyahi; ⏱ 8.30am-3.30pm & 6.30pm-2.30am

Still the most popular option along the Marina Walk, we like Chandelier for its *sheesha* and mezze rather than its main courses. While the service is somewhat relaxed, Chandelier is all about taking your time and chatting with friends while puffing on a water pipe.

🍴 EAUZONE *Fine Dining* $$$$

☎ 399 9999; One&Only Royal Mirage, Al-Sufouh Rd, Al-Mina al-Seyahi; 🕑 noon-3.30pm & 7.30-11.30pm

A romantic evening with adventurous cuisine awaits those making their way across the low-lit boardwalk to the tranquil pool-surrounded setting of this alluring restaurant – it's one best visited for dinner. The contemporary menu takes some Asian-inspired diversions, but never enough to break the spell of the magic surrounds.

🍴 INDEGO *Contemporary Indian* $$$$

☎ 399 8888; Grosvenor House, West Marina Beach; 🕑 7pm-midnight; Ⓥ

Although Dubai needs another upmarket Indian eatery like it needs more cranes, the gorgeous Indego distinguishes itself with the involvement of Vineet Bhatia, the first Indian chef to gain a Michelin star. While Vineet's not in the kitchen, his beautiful presentation (especially with the starters) and deft touch (the salmon tandoori is a revelation) sets Indigo apart.

Indian culinary masterpieces at Indego

Maya for margaritas and fresh Mexican tastes

🍴 MAYA *Mexican* $$$

☎ 399 5555; Le Royal Méridien Beach Resort & Spa; ☯ 12.30-4pm & 7.30pm-midnight Mon-Sat

As soon as you taste the *real* margaritas here, you know you're in safe hands. This whimsically designed restaurant gives Mexican cuisine the respect it deserves. Try the guacamole prepared fresh at your table, the amazing chilli *relleno* with seafood, or the humble tortilla soup, so authentic it would make a Mexican grandmother weep.

NEIGHBOURHOODS

NEW DUBAI

🍴 NINA *Contemporary Indian/ International* $$$

☎ 399 9999; Arabian Court, One&Only Royal Mirage, Al-Sufouh Rd, Al-Mina al-Seyahi; ⏱ 7-11.30pm

If you find the seductive orange-and-purple interior of Nina too mesmerising to concentrate on the menu, just order the tasting selection, soak up the sumptuous ambience and await the equally delicious fare that starts in India but then embarks on a global journey.

🍴 TAGINE *Moroccan* $$$$

☎ 399 9999; One&Only Royal Mirage, Al-Sufouh Rd, Al-Mina al-Seyahi; ⏱ 7-11pm

This long-standing restaurant admirably offers up the best Moroccan vibe in Dubai. Thankfully it also offers excellent versions of classics such as *harira* soup and pigeon *pastilla*. Meanwhile the tagine and couscous dishes will transport your taste buds directly to Fez. Thankfully, without the touts.

🍴 TANG *Modern European* $$$$

☎ 399 3333; Le Méridien Mina Seyahi Beach Resort & Marina, Al-Sufouh Rd, Jumeirah; ⏱ 7-11pm Sun-Fri

Dubai gets a taste of molecular gastronomy with this adventurous restaurant. Chef Stephane

Buchholzer is the most original and talented chef working in Dubai today and using fantastic ingredients (pork belly, Wagyu beef, scallops, langoustines) he creates a menu that challenges the senses. Just don't let the décor spoil the show.

🍸 DRINK

🍸 BAR 44 *Champagne Bar*

☎ 399 8888; Grosvenor House, West Marina Beach, New Dubai; ⏱ 6pm-2am

While this sophisticated champagne and cocktail bar, with spectacular views, has an exclusive clubby feel to it, the bar staff are

Divine interiors and international fare at Nina

friendly and regulars are made to feel like family. They may pride themselves on their champagne menu (and it is impressive) but their cocktails are sublime –Turquoise Blue is a heady potion, while the Mojito Martini is a revelation.

☒ BARASTI BAR *Outdoor Bar*
☎ 399 3333; Le Méridien Mina Seyahi Beach Resort & Marina, Al-Sufouh Rd, Jumeirah; ☾ 6pm-2am
Expanded in 2006 to add more deck area and palm-shaded terraces – with comfy rattan white-cushioned sofas and wooden benches – this enormous al fresco beachside bar still retains the laid-back atmosphere that first made it so popular with Dubai's residents. It's the perfect place to watch the sun go down with a drink on a balmy evening.

☒ BUDDHA BAR *DJ Bar*
☎ 399 8888; Le Méridien Grosvenor House, West Marina Beach, Jumeirah; ☾ 7pm-2am
Just like its sister bar in Paris, only more Shanghai than Thai, with the red chandeliers, hanging glass beads, Manchu-coated waiters, and a warren of exotic rooms, creating a mood of drama and intrigue. Add Oriental chill-out music, adventurous cocktails, and a buzzy vibe – book a table so you don't miss out.

☒ MAYA *Outdoor Bar*
☎ 399 5555; Le Royal Méridien Beach Resort & Spa; ☾ 6pm-2am
Dubai does al fresco bars so well and the rooftop bar of Dubai's best Mexican restaurant (see p106) is no exception. With cushioned banquette seating, sea views, and Mexican touches like the tiled fountain, you could be forgiven for thinking you're at Puerto Escondido or Play del Carmen, especially with a Margarita in hand, but that's what's so refreshing about it.

☒ MEDIA LOUNGE *Lounge Bar*
☎ 366 9111; Radisson SAS Hotel, Dubai Media City; ☾ 7.30am-1am
This hip café-bar is one of Dubai's coolest with its contemporary eclectic style and retro touches like gilt-edged mirrors and cow-hide cube ottomans. A regular crowd of Mac-book-clutching creative types from Media City make it their second home, using the funky space for coffee meetings and after-work drinks.

☒ THE ROOFTOP *Outdoor Bar*
☎ 399 9999; One&Only Royal Mirage, Al-Sufouh Rd, Al-Mina al-Seyahi; ☾ 5pm-1am
With its Persian carpets, cushioned banquettes and Moroccan lanterns, The Rooftop Bar is an *Arabian Nights'* fantasy. Add to

that a soundtrack of Oriental chill-out music and some of Dubai's best cocktails, and you have one of the city's most atmospheric bars. Book the romantic corner seat for special occasions.

☎ TAMANYA TERRACE
Outdoor Bar

☎ 366 9111; Radisson SAS Hotel, Dubai Media City; ⏱ 5pm-2am

The spectacular views at sunset as the lights from the skyscrapers of New Dubai go on are sufficient reason to settle in here for a drink, but locals love Friday's 'Favela Chic' night when Dubai's Latino community turn this rooftop lounge bar into a happening salsa club.

⭐ PLAY

☆ DUBAI AUTODROME
Racing Circuit

☎ 367 8700; www.dubaiautodrome.com; off Emirates Rd (take interchange 4 on Sheikh Zayed Rd), south of Dubai centre

Probably your best chance to witness some live motor sport (other than watching other drivers on their way from Dubai to Abu Dhabi) is the Dubai Autodrome. There's also a driving school and kart track at the course.

☆ EMIRATES GOLF CLUB
Golf Course

☎ 380 1999; www.dubaigolf.com; Interchange No 5, Sheikh Zayed Rd

If you're going to have a round of golf in Dubai (and if you're a golfer you should) challenge yourself on the same course used for the Dubai Desert Classic (www.dubaidesertclassic.com) and see if you can match Tiger Woods' tee shots. Home to the first grass course in the Middle East, the clubhouses, designed to resemble Bedouin tents, are quite striking.

☆ ORIENTAL HAMMAM *Spa*

☎ 399 9999; One&Only Royal Mirage, Al-Sufouh Rd, Al-Mina al-Seyahi; ⏱ 10am-9pm

This superb spa in the style of a traditional Moroccan or Turkish hammam is sublime. Opt for one of the traditional Oriental scrub, massage and spa treatments.

☆ SHEESHA COURTYARD
Sheesha Bar

☎ 399 9999; One&Only Royal Mirage, Al-Sufouh Rd, Al-Mina al-Seyahi; ⏱ 7pm-1am

It might take a connoisseur to appreciate all the different *sheesha* flavours on offer, but who wouldn't enjoy the aroma of apple *sheesha* reclining on cushions in this Arabian courtyard with palm trees flickering with fairy lights? See p19.

Cosmopolitan Dubai has plenty to offer, whether you're looking for local fashion designers or atmospheric souqs, fine-dining fusion cuisine or cheap street eats, laidback bars or thumping dance clubs, from snowboarding to camel rides.

Al Sarab, at Bab al-Shams Desert Resort & Spa, is perfect for sunset *sheesha* (p24)

ACCOMMODATION

Dubai is a city that has hotel stars in its eyes. Given its position as a luxury destination, as you go up in stars the properties get more and more lavish and, in many cases, offer better value. Business hotels such as Emirates Towers are world class, staying at the iconic Burj Al Arab (p23) earns you unlimited bragging rights, and a night at Mina A' Salam (opposite) is the stuff of *The Thousand and One Nights*. And there's plenty more to come – Dubai has a couple of dozen ostentatious four- and five-star properties due for completion before 2008.

The sheer number of hotels in Dubai appears daunting, but working out where to stay is straightforward. If your aim is to relax and catch some rays, stay at one of the five-star resorts along Jumeirah Beach. If you're interested in heritage, culture and souqs, the city hotels of Deira and Bur

haystack.lonelyplanet.com

Need a place to stay? Find and book it at www.lonely planet.com. More than 58 properties are featured for Dubai — each personally visited, thoroughly reviewed and happily recommended by a Lonely Planet author. From hostels to high-end hotels, we've hunted out the places that will bring you unique and special experiences. Read independent reviews by authors and other travel aficionados like you, and get practical information including amenities, maps and photos. Then reserve your room simply and securely via Haystack — our online booking service. It's all at www.lonelyplanet.com/accommodation.

Dubai will suit, with everything from one- to five-star hotels. If you're doing business in Dubai, there are excellent hotels in all parts of the city, but due to the traffic it's best to choose one close to where your meetings are.

Most hotels are kid-friendly and facilities offered are in line with other parts of the world; wheelchair access is generally excellent in the deluxe and top-end hotels; and all hotels listed have air conditioning.

Many people are shocked by some of the rack rates (standard full prices) quoted by hotels in Dubai. The reality is that you're unlikely to pay the published, high-season rack rates unless it's during one of Dubai's big events (see p27), conferences or trade shows. Being flexible about your dates or even taking a package deal can be rewarding as Dubai's hotels want high occupancy even if the rooms are going for a song. The best websites for online bookings are, of course, Lonely Planet's Haystack (www.lonelyplanet.com), as well as Expedia (www.expedia.com) and the hotel websites themselves, as many have a policy of offering the least expensive prices available.

BEST 1001 NIGHTS
> One&Only Royal Mirage (www.oneandonlyresorts.com)
> Mina A'Salam, Madinat Jumeirah (www.madinatjumeirah.com)
> Al Qasr, Madinat Jumeirah (www.madinatjumeirah.com)
> Park Hyatt Dubai (www.parkhyatt.com)
> XVA (www.xvagallery.com)

BEST BEACH RESORTS
> Le Royal Méridien Beach Resort (www.starwoodhotels.com/lemeridien)
> Le Méridien Mina Seyahi Resort (www.starwoodhotels.com/lemeridien)
> Jumeirah Beach Hotel (www.jumeirahbeachhotel.com)
> Ritz Carlton Hotel (www.ritz-carlton.com)
> Hilton Jumeirah Hotel (www.hilton.com)

BEST STYLISH SLEEPS
> Grosvenor House (www.starwoodhotels.com/lemeridien)
> Kempinski Mall of the Emirates (www.kempinski-dubai.com)
> Radisson SAS Dubai Media City (www.radissonsas.com)
> Hilton Dubai Creek (www.hilton.com)
> Qamardeen (www.qamardeenhotel.com)
> Emirates Towers (www.jumeirah emiratestowers.com)

BEST ON A BUDGET
> Orient Guest House (www.arabiancourtyard.com)
> Al Hijaz Heritage Motel (www.alhijazmotel.com)
> Ibis World Trade Centre (www.ibishotel.com)
> Baniyas Residence by Meridien (www.starwoodhotels.com/lemeridien)

Opposite Burj Al Arab peeks out from behind the extensive Madinat Jumeirah (p21)

CLUBS

To meet the insatiable demands of Dubai's cool young clubbing population, an increasing number of international DJs are racking up frequent flyer miles coming to Dubai. There's something on to suit all tastes every night of the week, from regular Deep Nights (www .deepnights.net) to one-off Hed Kandi (www.hedkandi.com) parties, and big-name DJs hitting Dubai every weekend – Axwell and Pete Tong, to name just a couple.

You'll hear all types of music spinning on Dubai's turntables – R&B, soul, funk, hip-hop, trance, tribal, electronica, drum'n'base and house in their myriad incarnations. An increasing fusion of Arabic, African, Indian, Latino and Euro styles is also emerging.

If you're only in town for a couple of nights and want to survey the scene, on Thursday night start a city-based night of clubbing at Ginseng (p67), before hitting Blush (p68) and our favourite, iBO (p53). On Friday night focus on the beach, starting at Sho Cho (p81), then Boudoir (p81), 360° (p78), The Apartment Lounge & Club (p81) and Trilogy (p83). You probably won't be going anywhere the next day.

Clubbers don't hit venues until late so expect to see lines forming around midnight. As clubs close around 3am, this means just a few hours on the dance floor, so the atmosphere can be intense. If you're 'not on the list' but want to avoid queues and don't mind propping up a bar for a while, arrive between 10pm and 11pm.

Thursday and Friday are the big nights out, but Saturdays can be good too. Check out *Time Out Dubai* magazine listings and pick up leaflets promoting events from cafés, bars and Virgin Megastore (p47), although serious clubbers should sign up to mailing lists before they leave home as tickets to the best DJs sell fast. The best sites are: 9714 for iBO (www.9714.com), Platinum List (www.platinumlistdubai.com), Mumtazz (www.mumtazz.com) and Peppermint Club (www.peppermint-club .com). Buy tickets for DJ events (and live concerts) online at www .itptickets.com or www.boxofficeme.com.

BEST FOR DJS
> iBO (p53)
> Trilogy (p53)
> 360° (p78)
> The Apartment (p81)

BEST PARTY CLUBS
> Blush (p68)
> Zinc (p99)
> Peppermint Club (p98)

Above An impressive DJ line-up pumps out international beats at Blush (p68)

FOOD

From tasty shwarma to credit card–maxing haute cuisine, Dubai doesn't lack breadth when it comes to dining. With the multicultural make-up of the city, you can indulge in just about any global cuisine that you desire. What Dubai's dining scene does lack, however, is depth when it comes to quality.

There is good news, though. While Gordon Ramsay's Verre has been schooling every wannabe haute cuisine joint in town about how to run a fine-dining restaurant, hotels are finally realising that it's important to satisfy an increasing foodie audience in Dubai. With more hotels on the way with big-name chefs attached, even an outpost of a celebrity chef is better than another anodyne eatery.

If you believe that any meal after breakfast should be accompanied by alcohol, hotels and sports clubs are your only option, so prepare to fly through more lobbies than an airline pilot during your stay.

But while the liquor-licensing laws are a major disincentive for entrepreneurial chefs wanting to operate outside the five-star confines, cafés and restaurants in Dubai's malls are becoming more sophisticated. You will find that excellent new eateries such as Almaz by Momo (p93) and

Emporio Armani Caffé (p94) are head and shoulders above most hotel restaurants.

Out on the streets, the corner restaurants serving up lashings of expat cuisines such as Indian and Pakistani keep the workers (and travellers) sated – just look for the busiest ones. Samosas and sweet tea are heaven-sent if you're exploring the souqs and a street shwarma and fresh mango juice is the perfect pick-me-up while comparing gold prices. And isn't the experience better than a boring hotel buffet?

BEST GOURMET EXPERIENCES
> Verre by Gordon Ramsay (p50)
> Café Chic (p47)
> Maya (p106)
> Tang (p107)
> Nina (p107)

BEST MIDDLE EASTERN
> Tagine (p107)
> Almaz by Momo (p93)
> Awtar (p63)
> Shahrzad (p49)

BEST FOR ATMOSPHERE
> Eauzone (p105)
> Pierchic (p77)
> Indego (p105)
> Mumtaz Mahal (p65)
> Kan Zaman (p64)

BEST CHEAP EATS
> Noodle House (p94)
> Chopstix (p48)
> Bella Donna (p77)
> Al Mallah (p76)

Opposite Bella Donna's service staff get ready to impress (p77) **Above** Moroccan favourite, Tagine (p107)

V

ARCHITECTURE

Dubai's architecture is eclectic and audacious. The city's anything-is-possible attitude has resulted in some of the world's most attention-grabbing edifices. The iconic Burj Al Arab (p23) tops everybody's list of sights to tick off, however its low-rise neighbour, Madinat Jumeirah (p21), with its Arabian-inspired architecture is equally as compelling.

While Madinat Jumeirah looks back to the multistorey buildings of Jeddah in Saudi Arabia, in the Bastakiya Quarter (p12) of Bur Dubai the wind towers signal Dubai's own Persian-influenced style. There were two types of traditional house here – the *masayf*, a summer house incorporating a wind tower, and the *mashait*, a winter house with a courtyard. Along with these residential styles there were three other types of traditional architecture: religious (mosques), defensive (forts and watchtowers) and commercial (souqs). Readily available materials, such as gypsum and coral from offshore reefs and banks of the Creek were put to use.

Today, concrete, steel and glass towers dominate the skyline and the headlines in Dubai. Whether it's the loopiest new project, such as a solar-powered rotating skyscraper, or the progress reports of the world's tallest building – Burj Dubai (www.burjdubai.com) is currently moving skyward at a rate of a new floor every four days – Dubai is architecturally daring.

BEST HERITAGE ARCHITECTURE
> Bastakiya Quarter (p12)
> Shindagha area (p13)
> Heritage House & Al-Ahmadiya School (p25)
> Majlis Ghorfat Um Al-Sheef (p74)
> Bait Al Wakeel (p14)

BEST DUBAI CREEK ARCHITECTURE
> National Bank of Dubai (p40)
> Dubai Creek Golf & Yacht Club (p53)
> Hilton Dubai Creek (p113)

BEST SHEIKH ZAYED RD BUILDINGS
> World Trade Centre (p84)
> Emirates Towers (p113)
> Dusit Dubai (p84)
> Burj Dubai (above)

BEST JUMEIRAH ARCHITECTURE
> Burj Al Arab (p23)
> Jumeirah Beach Hotel (p113)
> Madinat Jumeirah (p21)
> Jumeirah Mosque (p20)

BARS

Dubai is a cosmopolitan city and its bars are as cool as they come, fusing exotic Eastern and contemporary Western styles in their drinks, design and music.

For those who like their watering holes low-key, there are typical English pubs and Irish bars, with Guinness on tap, memorabilia-filled walls and boozy regulars propping up the bar.

But if you're only in town for a short stay, check out the bars that Dubai does best, including the Oriental atmosphere of The Rooftop (p108), the hip style of 1897 (p96) and the stunning views of Vu's (p96).

For those who don't like to mix their drinks, try one of Dubai's many specialist bars, such as Bar 44 (p107) for champagne, The Agency (p78) for wine, or The Terrace (p52) for vodka.

Dubai residents often begin their night with a sunset drink at a laidback waterside spot before kicking on to a buzzy city bar and something more clubby later on. With endless options for drinking, the nights can be long. Some bars open around noon, while others don't start until 6pm. The early openers tend to close around midnight, while those starting later don't shut until 2am or 3am. Check out *Time Out Dubai* and *What's On* magazines for the latest happy hour and drinks promotions.

BEST SEA BREEZES
> Sho Cho (p81)
> The Rooftop (p108)
> Bahri Bar (p78)
> Maya (p108)

BEST VISTAS
> Skyview Bar (p81)
> Tamanya Terrace (p109)
> The Terrace (p52)
> Après (p97)

BEST FOR BUZZY ATMOSPHERE
> Buddha Bar (p108)
> The Agency (p96)
> Ginseng (p67)
> Vu's Bar (p97)

BEST COCKTAIL/CHAMPAGNE BARS
> Bar 44 (p107)
> 1897 Bar (p96)
> Cin Cin's (p97)
> Lotus One (p97)

SNAPSHOTS

BEACHES

Dubai's locals love their beaches. While Jumeirah residents living within splashing distance of the crystal-clear turquoise waters make it a daily ritual to head down to the beach for early-morning swims or late-afternoon walks, the rest of us make an effort to hit the beach on weekends. Even Dubai's guest workers get down there on a Friday, when you'll see construction company buses waiting at Open Beach while workers play cricket on the sand.

Dubai's verdant beach parks are also popular, as much for family barbecues as for swimming and sunbathing opportunities. While there is an entry fee, the beaches are clean and patrolled by lifeguards and the facilities (change rooms, kiosks and kids' playgrounds) are excellent.

Although the Palm Island developments have blotted the horizon, the beach resorts along the Jumeirah stretch (pictured below) are some of the best in the world, with enormous swimming pools, wet bars, palm-filled gardens, and excellent water sports and activities. Fortunately, you don't have to stay at a hotel to enjoy its beach, as many resorts run beach clubs with daily and weekly access. See p113 for best beach resorts.

BEST FREE BEACHES
> Umm Suqeim Beach (p83)
> Open Beach (p83)
> Kite Beach (p82)

BEST BEACH PARKS & CLUBS
> Jumeirah Beach Park (p82)
> Al-Mamzar Park (p41)
> One&Only Royal Mirage (p113)
> Le Royal Méridien Beach Resort (p113)
> Jumeirah Beach Hotel (p113)

BOARD SPORTS

With abundant sand, surf, concrete and snow (!) Dubai has become an unlikely board-sport mecca. When the wind blows down Jumeirah Beach, the local kite-surfing fraternity hit Kite Beach (pictured below; p82). Hoping for lesser winds are the dedicated band of expat surfers who hit the clean, small waves at Umm Suqeim (p83) during the winter months.

The city's concrete jungle is perfect for skateboarding, apart from the officious rent-a-cops. However, on any given weekend there's usually a street session at Open Beach (p83). You can wakeboard at the beach resorts, but head to The Wakeboard School if you want to get serious.

Dubai affords you the opportunity to try the least forgiving of the board sports, sandboarding. Sand offers more friction than snow and it's harder to master than snowboarding, but why is it the least forgiving? If you face plant, eating snow is way better than eating sand.

And speaking of snowboarding, Dubai's indoor snow park, Ski Dubai (p98), has a quad lift and a pretty decent 400m run with a black section. However, the best time to visit is freestyle night, when the music's pumping and the kids are jumping. Dubai's board-sport culture is thriving.

BEST BOARD SPORT LINKS

> Dubai Kite Club (www.dubaikite club.com)
> Surfers of Dubai (www.surfersof dubai.com)
> The Wakeboard School (www .thewakeboardschool.com)
> Desert Rangers (www.desertrangers .com, for sandboarding)
> Ski Dubai (www.skidxb.com)

DESERT ESCAPES

There's nothing like experiencing the desert, and Dubai residents, locals and expats alike, frequently make an effort to get out of the city and onto the emirate's sand-swept roads. Whether it's for a drive for some camel spotting, a weekend of camping or a few days relaxing at a dreamy resort (see p24), it's amazing how some time in the desert can clear the head.

For travellers on short trips to Dubai, an organized 4WD desert safari is the most popular way to experience the Arabian sands. Nothing to be embarrassed about, expats look forward to family and friends coming to stay so they have an excuse to go too.

Desert safaris are a great way to experience the emirate's rugged terrain and sublime desert scenery while ticking off a few must-do activities. Leaving Dubai in the afternoon so you can watch the sunset over the desert from the back of a camel, you get to experience some exhilarating desert driving (known locally as 'dune-bashing') on the way to a Bedouin-style campsite. Once there you can try sandboarding, do that camel ride, get a henna design, enjoy an Arabic barbecue dinner, and have a shimmy with a belly dancer. Some tour companies also offer overnight trips, which we highly recommend – nothing beats sleeping in the desert under the stars. Sublime.

BEST DESERT ACTIVITIES
> Dune-bashing
> Sunset camel ride
> Hot-air ballooning
> Sandboarding
> Sleeping under the stars

BEST DESERT HIDEAWAYS
> Al Maha Desert Resort & Spa (www
  .al-maha.com)
> Bab al-Shams Desert Resort & Spa
  (www.jumeirahbabalshams.com)

BEST TOUR COMPANIES
> Arabian Adventures (www.arabian
  -adventures.com)
> Off-Road Adventures (www.arabian
  tours.com)
> Net Tours (www.nettoursdubai.com)
> Balloon Adventures Dubai (www
  .ballooning.ae)

MUSEUMS & GALLERIES

Dubai's museum scene is small, which may be perfect for those who want guilt-free days on the sand, but has art-loving residents counting down the days until they fly off to get their culture fix.

Nevertheless, the few museums on offer here are excellent. They're small and manageable so you'll rarely spend more than an hour browsing yet will come away with an amazing insight into Dubai's history, culture and crazy development that you wouldn't otherwise get. The best, Dubai Museum (p11), is a must, providing a comprehensive introduction to the city that will make your experience all the more meaningful.

Art-lovers should devote a few hours to some gallery hopping. Dubai has a small but growing art scene and there are some outstanding commercial galleries specialising in adventurous contemporary Middle East art – you're likely to be impressed by what you see, and original art also makes a unique souvenir. Make The Third Line (p88) and B21 (p85) a priority, followed by the Bastakiya Quarter galleries XVA (p59) and Majlis Gallery (p58).

Most galleries hang new shows every few weeks, often with buzzy champagne openings, which offer a great chance to meet like-minded locals. Check Canvas Guide (www.canvasonline.com) for upcoming exhibitions and sign up to gallery websites before you leave home.

BEST MUSEUMS
> Dubai Museum (p11)
> Sheikh Saeed al-Maktoum House (p58)
> Heritage House (p25)
> Al-Ahmadiya School (p25)
> Majlis Ghorfat Um-al-Sheef (p74)

BEST ART GALLERIES
> The Third Line (p88)
> XVA (p59)
> Majlis Gallery (p58)
> Art Space (p85)
> B21 Gallery (p85)

BEST ART EVENTS
> Sharjah Biennial, April (www.sharjah biennial.org/en)
> Gulf Art Fair, March (www.gulfart fair.com)
> The Creek Contemporary Art Fair, March (www.9714.com)

SHEESHA CAFÉS

Sheesha is one of the most chilled-out of Dubai's essential experiences and unlike cigarette smoke, the smell of the flavoured tobacco sees even nonsmokers enjoying the ambient *sheesha* cafés.

Popular with Emiratis as much as Dubai's many Middle Eastern expats, *sheesha* cafés provide a perfect opportunity for some excellent people-watching and a chance to meet locals in a relaxed environment without the impediments of loud music and alcohol (few Emiratis will talk to you while you're nursing a brew).

While it's hard to beat the enchanting Arabian setting of the Sheesha Courtyard (p109), you'll find an equally exotic vibe at Almaz by Momo (p93), which is popular with Emiratis because it is not licensed, and Kan Zaman (p64), which sees Arab expat families filling its tables most evenings.

Less focused on atmosphere and more on music and views is Tamanya Terrace (p109), which sees Arab and European creative types from Media City puffing its pipes. A beautiful young Arab expat crowd fills the comfy sofas at Fudo (p77) late most nights, while QDs (p53) attracts a regular set of British and Aussie expats swigging back beers with their *sheesha*.

BEST ATMOSPHERE
> Sheesha Courtyard (p109)
> Almaz by Momo (pictured right; p93)
> Kan Zaman (p64)
> Souq Madinat Jumeirah (p76)

BEST AL FRESCO
> QD's (p53)
> Tamanya Terrace (p109)
> Fudo (p77)
> Kan Zaman (p64)

SHOPPING MALLS

Maligned elsewhere, shopping malls make sense in the stifling heat of Dubai. Malls have become like town squares in other cities – complete with central plaza, fountain, entertainment stage and souvenir-laden barrows – giving travellers a glimpse into Dubai's social culture and an opportunity to mingle with locals. Older folk sit at a café watching the world go by while younger ones send text messages to each other as they cruise around. Ibn Battuta (see p101) takes the concept to the extreme, with specialised shopping 'streets' resembling market places in 14th-century Andalusia, Tunisia, Egypt, Persia, India and China.

Shopping is a daily ritual for Emiratis, but in Dubai it's taken to a sublime level. Elegant Dubaian women, designer *shaylas* (women's head scarves) dripping with Swarovski crystals, treat a trip to Saks (p60) as their burqa-wearing mothers might a morning at the spice souq. They take their time, make their choice, scrutinise the product, then, when they're ready to buy – always ask for a discount. Do the same.

Duty-free shopping doesn't necessarily imply the lower prices it does elsewhere because the UAE is blissfully tax-free, but always shop around and ask for 'the best price'. Shopping in Dubai is most fun at night when locals shop. Malls generally open 10am to 10pm daily, except Friday when they open in the afternoon.

BEST MALLS
> Deira City Centre (p46)
> Mall of the Emirates (p92)
> BurJuman Centre (p60)
> Ibn Battuta Mall (p101)
> Mercato Mall (p75)

BEST MULTI-BRAND STORES
> Villa Moda (p93)
> Aizone (p90)
> Harvey Nichols (p91)
> Saks Fifth Avenue (p60)
> Faces (p60)

BEST INDIE BOUTIQUES
> Amzaan (p60)
> Five Green (p60)
> Ginger & Lace (p101)
> Bauhaus (p101)
> S*uce (p75)

BEST FOR SOUVENIRS
> Lata's (p74)
> Al-Orooba Oriental (p59)
> National Iranian Carpets (p75)
> Pride of Kashmir (p75)
> Al-Jaber Gallery (p90)

SOUQS

In contrast to the sleek, shiny, squeaky-clean shopping malls, the cacophony, colour and chaos of the souqs is what makes them so appealing.

Neither the breezy wooden arcades of Bur Dubai Souq (p14) nor the ramshackle shops of Deira's Covered Souq (p41) resemble the *barasti* roofed bazaar that was established on the banks of Dubai Creek in the 1830s, but the city's souqs remain full of character and still have the reputation as the best in Arabia.

Dubai's souqs hold everything imaginable – you'll find Arabian perfume, traditional *kandouras* (white robes), spices and bellydancing costumes. Most shops specialise in something, but some seem to sell everything, ancient and modern, from pumice stones to traditional wooden tooth cleaners.

Whatever you buy, make sure to bargain, and in between bargaining take time to chat to the sales guys – they hail from everywhere: Mumbai, Islamabad, Isfahan and even Kiev. Accept all offers of tea – the socialising is as much fun as the shopping. And the shoppers are just as varied – you'll see foreign tourists haggling over suitcases and local ladies looking for the latest textiles.

Souqs are generally open from Saturday to Thursday 10am to 1pm, shutting for lunch and siesta, and reopening around 5pm until 10pm. On Friday (prayer day) they open in the afternoon.

BEST SOUQS
> Deira Gold Souq (p17)
> Bur Dubai Souq (p14)
> Deira Covered Souq (p41)
> Deira Spice Souq (pictured above; p16)
> Souq Madinat Jumeirah (p21)

BEST SOUVENIRS
> Embroidered curly toed Aladdin slippers
> Frankincense and *oud* (fragrant wood)
> *Sheesha* pipe set
> Henna design kit
> Arabian *attars* or perfumes

SPAS

A weekly pampering is an essential part of life for many expats and an increasing number of visitors to Dubai are adding a spa treatment to their 'to-do' list right after the suntan and shopping.

While there are tranquil Zen-minimalist spas and exotic Moroccan- and Turkish-style hammams such as Oriental Hammam, what Dubai does best is the extravagant luxury spa with ornate pillars, gold leaf and big sunken baths. Naturally, no one can top the Burj Al Arab – its Assawan Spa is a must.

Most spas have a long menu of classic treatments, ranging from facials, exfoliations, scrubs, soaks, wraps and massages to the much-hyped hot-oil Ayurvedic therapies. However, we prefer the more innovative spa packages that are very in tune with the lifestyle (Jet Lag Recovery, anyone?) and culture (yes, we'll take the Cleopatra recipe milk bath).

Themed packages are the most fun and usually include a combination scrub, bath, massage and facial, along with use of the steam room and wet area, herbal teas, juices and a healthy lunch. They might range from a 90-minute treatment to a more indulgent full day at the spa. Better add that day to the itinerary now.

BEST SPAS
> Assawan Spa – Burj Al Arab (p71)
> Oriental Hammam – One&Only Royal Mirage (pictured right; p113)
> Cleopatra's Spa – Wafi City Pharoah's Club (p68)
> Kempinski Softtouch Spa – Kempinski, Mall of the Emirates Hotel (p98)

BEST SPA TREATMENTS
> Around the World massage – Assawan Spa (p71)
> Ritual of the Orient – Oriental Hammam (p109)
> Cleopatra's Wrap – Cleopatra's Spa (p68)
> Tranquillity Treatment – Kempinski Softtouch Spa (p98)

SPORTS EVENTS

Dubai's winter months are tailor-made for outdoor sporting events and the city obliges by holding an excellent roster of international events. The love of horses running deep in Arab blood is best represented by the Dubai International Racing Carnival (February through March) culminating in the Dubai World Cup, the world's richest horse race. There's no gambling, but the entertaining crowd action is a sure bet.

Also not lacking for prize money is the Dubai Desert Classic golf tournament, attracting some of the world's best golfers. Taking place in late February or March at the Emirates Golf Club, golf-crazy expats take the week off to watch the world's best go round their local course.

The Dubai Tennis Championships, held over two weeks from late February, consists of a Women's Tennis Association (WTA) event followed by an Association of Tennis Professionals (ATP) event. The tournament now attracts the best names from both circuits and the size of the stadium makes it a great opportunity to see freakish talents like Federer up close.

The most social event of Dubai's sporting calendar, the Dubai Rugby Sevens tournament, sees many of Dubai's expats worshipping the sport of drinking beer outdoors. Apparently, it's also a rugby competition. Book early.

BEST SPORTING EVENTS

> Dubai World Cup (www.dubaiworld cup.com)
> Dubai Tennis Championships (www .dubaitennischampionships.com)
> Dubai Desert Classic (www.dubai desertclassic.com)
> Dubai Rugby Sevens (www .dubairugby7s.com)
> Dubai Marathon (www.dubai marathon.org)

BEST SPORTING VENUES

> Emirates Golf Club (www.dubaigolf .com)
> Nad al-Sheba Racing Club (www .nadalshebaclub.com)
> Dubai Autodrome (www.dubaiauto drome.com)
> Dubai Exiles Rugby Club (www .dubaiexiles.com)

A young boy at a Bedouin wedding at the Heritage Village (p13)

BACKGROUND

HISTORY

RECENT EVENTS

The most significant events in Dubai's recent history were the discovery of oil in 1966 and its exportation from 1969, setting in place the foundations for an extraordinarily rapid development that continues to the present day.

Before Britain left the Arabian Peninsula in 1968, it attempted to create a new state encompassing the Trucial States (most of which is today's United Arab Emirates, or UAE), Bahrain and Qatar. While Bahrain and Qatar opted to pursue their own independence, the leaders of Abu Dhabi and Dubai committed to forming a single state and the UAE was born on 2 December 1971, consisting of Dubai, Abu Dhabi, Ajman, Fujairah, Sharjah and Umm al-Qaiwain; Ras al-Khaimah joined in 1972. The emirs approved a formula whereby Abu Dhabi and Dubai (respectively) would have the most responsibility and power in the federation, leaving each emir in control of his own emirate. Sheikh Zayed of Abu Dhabi became the president of the UAE and Sheikh Rashid of Dubai became vice president.

After Sheikh Rashid died in 1990 following a long illness, he was succeeded by his eldest son, Sheikh Maktoum bin Rashid al-Maktoum, who had been regent during his father's illness. Sheikh Maktoum steered a steady course for Dubai until his death in January 2006, when the third son of the dynasty, the ambitious Sheikh Mohammed bin Rashid al-Maktoum took over. For more on the ruling family, see p132.

EARLY HISTORY

Archaeological remains around Dubai show evidence of human presence as far back as 8000 BC. Until 3000 BC the area supported nomadic herders who fished on the coast during winter and relocated inland during summer. Agriculture developed with the cultivation of date palms around 2500 BC, providing food and materials for building and weaving.

The Sassanids, who ruled Persia from AD 224 to AD 636, occupied the area until the Umayyads supplanted them in the 7th century. They brought the Arabic language with them, uniting the region with the

Islamic world. During this period, maritime trade in the Gulf expanded thanks to the region's strategic location on major trade routes between the Mediterranean and the Indian Ocean.

EUROPEAN PRESENCE
In the late 16th century Portugal became the first European power to take control of the region's lucrative trade routes with India and the Far East. Dispirited by the monopolistic, well-armed Portuguese invasion, the local tribes sought refuge in landlocked oases, such as Liwa and Al-Ain.

The French and the Dutch invaded the area in the 17th and 18th centuries, aspiring to control the trading routes to the east. The British were equally intent on protecting the sea route to India, and in 1766 the Dutch gave way to Britain's East India Company, which had established Gulf trading links in 1616.

THE TRUCIAL COAST
Following the move of the powerful Bani Yas tribe from the Liwa Oasis to Abu Dhabi in 1833, and the death of Sheikh Tanoun in a coup, a political split resulted, leading Maktoum bin Butti to take about 800 members of the ambitious Al Falasah branch to Dubai. Settling on the creek of Bur Dubai their weight in numbers gave them immediate control over the city.

Throughout the 19th century Dubai remained an enclave of fishermen, pearl divers and Bedouin, Indian and Persian merchants. In 1892, the British reinforced their power through 'exclusive agreements' (or truces – hence the term Trucial Coast) with the sheikhs. In 1894, Dubai's ruler, Sheikh Maktoum bin Hasher al-Maktoum, exempted foreign traders from paying taxes, and created the free port of Dubai that exists to this day.

THE EXPANDING CITY
By the turn of the 20th century, Dubai was a well-established town with a population of about 10,000 and, despite some lean years after the collapse of the vitally important pearling industry in 1929, its significance as a trading hub continued to increase. In 1951 the Trucial States Council was founded, bringing together the leaders of what would become the UAE.

THE RULING FAMILY

Power in Dubai rests with the ruling Al-Maktoum family. Though the UAE has a federal government, each emir is sovereign within his own emirate. The Maktoums have ruled Dubai since 1833, when they moved from the Liwa Oasis, with recent rulers Sheikh Rashid bin Saeed al-Maktoum (ruling 1958–1990) and Sheikh Maktoum bin Rashid al-Maktoum (ruling 1990–2006) presiding over the dawn of Dubai's golden period. While their leadership was steady and focussed on ensuring that the place didn't return to being a minor trading hub after the oil ran out, current ruler Sheikh Mohammed bin Rashid al-Maktoum is pushing the city to places previously thought unimaginable.

Always destined to take over leadership of Dubai, Sheikh Mohammed has long been the most visible and charismatic face of the ruling family. Equestrian, soldier, poet and all-round overachiever, Sheikh Mohammed has been behind most of the city's most attention-grabbing projects, including the Burj Al Arab, Internet City, Media City and the Shopping Festival. While these projects might appear disparate, they are all based around one theme – getting people to visit or move to Dubai and spend money. From the early 1990s Sheikh Mohammed planned to make the city a premiere tourism destination. Realising that every great city had an iconic symbol, such as the Empire State Building or the Eiffel Tower, he set about creating Dubai's with the Burj Al Arab. In the late 1990s, while many governments were wondering why they didn't control the internet, Sheikh Mohammed was already putting in place an 'e-government' strategy requiring all the city's government services to be available online within 12 months. And they were.

Sheikh Maktoum's decisiveness and desire for rapid change has seen fantastic benefits for the economy, and there's no longer talk about Dubai disappearing into the sands when the oil runs out. Moving from a developing state to a successful multicultural metropolis in the space of a generation, however, has left many residents shell-shocked, locked in horrific traffic jams, or having to march down Sheikh Zayed Rd to get paid by dubious building firms creating the future of Dubai. The most fascinating thing, though, is that this ambitious sheikh notes that he's only achieved one-tenth of what he's setting out to accomplish – he wants Dubai, the UAE and the Arab world to become world leaders in whatever they set out to do.

TAKING BACK THE DESERT

While Dubai might appear to be more interested in theme parks than national parks, the emirate's largest project to date has actually involved rehabilitation of the desert, sponsored by an unlikely partner. Al Maha Desert Resort & Spa (p24) opened in 1999 on land owned by Emirates Airlines and its success led to an environmental audit in 2000. A conservation proposal was approved in 2002, and the Dubai Desert Conservation Reserve (DDCR) now encompasses nearly 5% of Dubai emirate.

The DDCR's replanting of native flora has enabled Arabian oryx (a large variety of antelope) to be reintroduced along with several other species. The result has been a stunning success and it's heartening that Dubai has an attraction whose appeal is in simply watching herds of graceful oryxes graze.

If you don't stay at Al Maha but still want to get out in the desert, make sure to use one of the approved operators; see p122.

ECONOMY

Dubai is the second-richest emirate in the UAE after Abu Dhabi, but its dwindling oil and gas reserves make up only 6% of its GDP. Dubai prudently uses that revenue to create the infrastructure for trade, manufacturing and tourism. The services sector, which includes tourism and tourism-related industries such as restaurants, has been growing at an annual rate of 21% since 2000 and now provides nearly 74% of the emirate's GDP.

Growth in GDP terms has been phenomenal, with Dubai recording a growth rate of around 13% per annum since 2000, exceeding the widely-publicised emerging economies of China and India. Much of this growth has been led by government-backed and -owned initiatives in which a subsidiary of the state partners with private companies, thereby encouraging foreign investment. With its attractive tax breaks and infrastructure, Dubai has proved itself to be very successful in enticing global companies to make the city their headquarters in the Middle East.

The city's per capita income was Dh114,362 per annum (about US$31,300) at the time of research, a figure that would come as a surprise to expat labourers sweating it out for Dh500 to Dh1000 a month, and growth has been around 6% per annum for the last few years. Although it is unlikely that we will see Emiratis competing for bricklaying duties anytime in the near future, the government has made attempts to 'Emiratise' the workforce. It is encouraging more nationals to enter the workforce and it has imposed quotas to employ local workers in some industries.

While many analysts believe that Dubai has expanded too far too fast, and that its economy is heading for trouble, others believe the city has a sufficiently sturdy economic base to survive any bumps in the road – such as worrying inflation levels and shortage of housing. This could perhaps be Sheikh Mohammed's greatest challenge in the years ahead.

MULTICULTURALISM

Dubai is one of the most multicultural cities on the planet, with expats from over 160 countries comprising an estimated 90% of Dubai's roughly 1.4 million people. As a result, you will find a fabulous fusion of food, fashion and music on the streets – from East African textiles in Naif Rd Souq to Bollywood music in Bur Dubai – and as many different lifestyles being played out as there are grains of sand on Jumeirah Beach.

The first expats were mostly conservative Sunnis and Shiites from southern Iran who built the Bastakiya neighbourhood in the 1930s, until the 1980 Islamic revolution when a more affluent class arrived. Now, some 400,000 Iranians live and work here. Arab expats comprise around 15% of the population, mainly coming from Lebanon, Syria, Jordan, Egypt and Iraq. Many have been here since the 1970s and their children were born in the UAE – these young people are responsible for some of the most exciting art, culture, fashion and music being created in Dubai.

Western expats make up the smallest percentage at around 5%. Once a predominantly British contingent, now continental Europeans, Australians, Canadians and South Africans join them in enjoying the good life.

The majority of Dubai's expats, comprising almost 60%, are Indian. They supply the city with much of its cheap labour, as well as filling IT, management and professional positions. Many, along with Filipinos, Sri Lankans, Indonesians and Malaysians, work Dubai's massive services sector. All make more money here than at home and they work hard six days a week.

Bangladeshis, Pakistanis, Afghanis and Chinese workers go about the hazardous business of construction in Dubai, working gruelling

MYTHBUSTING

You can buy alcohol.
As a visitor, you can buy drinks in bars and clubs (generally attached to four- and five-star hotels). But you can't buy alcohol to take back to your hotel – so stock up on duty free on the way into Dubai. Non-Muslim expats need an alcohol licence, entitling them to a fixed monthly fix of alcohol (the more you earn, the higher your limit) available from low-key liquor outlets.

You can't wear whatever you want.
All that locals ask is that visitors dress respectfully, with clothes that are not too revealing. Locals will judge you on how you dress; boys in shorts at shopping malls will be assumed to have forgotten their pants and girls who reveal too much skin will cause offence. If you're going clubbing, take a taxi.

Homosexuality is not banned.
Simply being homosexual is not illegal as such, but homosexual acts are – as are any sex acts outside of marriage.

Holding hands in public is OK.
The guys you see holding hands in Dubai are simply displaying a sign of friendship. It's okay for married couples to hold hands as well, but serious public displays of affection by couples (married or not) are frowned upon and fines and jail terms can result.

Dubai is not the capital of the UAE.
Abu Dhabi is the capital of the UAE. Both are emirates (like states) and both are the capitals of their respective state, but Abu Dhabi is the seat of UAE power. It just looks like Dubai is the capital, because Dubai acts like it's the capital.

12-hour shifts, six days a week, and living in labour camps provided by construction companies. While conditions are improving, the heat can be oppressive and the pressure to complete Dubai's sleek skyscrapers is enormous.

At the opposite end of the pay scales are the wealthy, professional, management classes – once Western, now increasingly Arab, Iranian and Indian – with big salary packages, nice cars, a big villa with maid and nanny. Their wives (nearly all of these managers are male), with little left to do at home, spend much of their time with other women in similar circumstances – these 'Jumeirah Janes', as the expat community refers to them, keep the cosmetics and spa industries alive and the coffee shops ticking over during the day.

RELIGION

Islam is the official religion of the UAE, with Sunnis comprising around 90% of Muslims and Shiite making up the rest. The government gives all mosques guidance on religious sermons and monitors them for political content. The UAE follows a tolerant version of Shari'a law (alongside civil law) although Shiite can pursue Shiite law cases through a special council rather than Shari'a courts. The country also has large numbers of expatriate Hindus, Sikhs and Christians who can practice their religion freely, although Dubai is the only emirate with Hindu temples and a Sikh Gurdwara.

Be prepared to be woken early each morning by the haunting call to prayer, especially if you stay in the older parts of Bur Dubai and Deira. At the first sign of dawn, you'll hear a cacophony of sounds as muezzins chant the call through speakers on the minarets of each mosque. Before speakers were used, the muezzins used to climb a ladder up to the minarets and call

THE FIVE PILLARS OF ISLAM

> **Shahadah** The profession of faith: 'There is no god but God, and Mohammed is the messenger of God.'

> **Salat** Muslims are required to pray five times every day: at dawn, noon, mid-afternoon, sunset and twilight. During prayers Muslims perform a series of prostrations while facing the Kaaba, the ancient shrine at the centre of the Grand Mosque in Mecca. Before a Muslim can pray, he or she must perform a series of ritual ablutions, and if water isn't available for this, sand or soil is substituted.

> **Zakat** Muslims must give part of their income to help the poor. The operation of this practice has varied over time: either it was seen as an individual duty or the state collected it as a form of income tax to be redistributed through mosques or religious charities.

> **Sawm** It was during the holy month of Ramadan that Mohammed received his first revelation in AD 610. Muslims mark this event by fasting from sunrise until sunset throughout Ramadan, during which smoking and sex are also forbidden. Young children, travellers and those in poor health are exempt from fasting, though those who are able to are supposed to make up the days they missed at a later time.

> **Hajj** All able Muslims are required to make the pilgrimage to Mecca at least once in their lifetime, if possible, during a specific few days in the first and second weeks of the Muslim month of Dhul Hijja. Visiting Mecca and performing the prescribed rituals at any other time of the year is also considered spiritually desirable, and such visits are called *umrah,* or 'little pilgrimages'.

out from the top. If someone can't get to a mosque, they can stop wherever they are to pray – in hotel lobbies, in shops, parks, even by the side of the road, as long as they face Mecca. You'll notice a qibla (an arrow that indicates the direction of Mecca) in your hotel room, either on the ceiling, desk or bedside table.

The phrase that you'll be able to make out most during the call to prayer is *Allah-u-akbar*, which means 'God is Great'. The morning call to prayer is slightly different from the others, when the gently nudging extra line *As-salaatu khayrun min al nawn* (it is better to pray than to sleep) is repeated.

ARTS

VISUAL ARTS

Dubai's visual arts scene is flourishing (also see p123). Just five years ago most art shown in established commercial galleries was created by Western expats. These days the most interesting work exhibited is by Emirati and other Middle Eastern artists. In the past, themes reflected the history and heritage of Dubai (watercolours of the Bastakiya were popular) whereas now increasing numbers of artists are experimenting in abstract and mixed-media forms that appropriate aspects of Emirati, Arab or Persian culture in a playful, provocative way. Female Emirati artists continue to garner well-deserved praise, including Ragdha Bukhash and Lamya Gargash, while credit for the invigoration of the arts scene goes to the young curators of Dubai's more adventurous galleries, such as The Third Line (see p88), and Sheikha Hoor al-Qasimi, director of the excellent Sharjah International Biennial (p123).

> **ART, CULTURE & FASHION IN PRINT**
> * *Alef* – Dubai's version of *Vogue* with hints of *Wallpaper*
> * *Bidoun* – cutting-edge culture from the Arab diaspora
> * *Sourah* – design and photography from young Emiratis
> * *Viva* – a glossy cross between *Elle* and *Cosmopolitan*

POETRY & LITERATURE

There is some wonderful Arabic-language literature, yet little is available in English. Only two short-story anthologies by prolific Emirati writer Mohammed al-Murr, *The Wink of the Mona Lisa and Other Stories from the*

ESSENTIAL DUBAI READS

> *Arabian Destiny* – Edward Henderson
> *Father of Dubai: Sheikh Rashid bin Saeed Al-Maktoum* – Graeme Wilson
> *Telling Tales: An Oral History of Dubai* – Julia Wheeler
> *The Wells of Memory, An Autobiography* – Easa Saleh Al-Gurg
> *The Wink of the Mona Lisa* – Mohammad Al-Murr

Gulf and *Dubai Tales*, have been translated. Iranian expat Marian Behnam's *Heirloom: Evening Tales from the East* retells folk tales from the 1920s to 1940s, translated from Bastaki, her mother tongue. There is also a lively children's literature scene, with Julia Johnson's delightful illustrated books, such as *A is for Arabia,* readily available. But it's poetry that permeates the cultural, intellectual and everyday life of Emiratis. In Bedouin culture, poetry is prized and Emiratis spontaneously recite it with their friends at social occasions and public events. Young people publish their own poetry, particularly romantic poems, on websites and in magazines. There are scores of well-known local male poets, as well as a handful of female poets, who like to experiment with classical Arabic poetry. The Jebel Ali Palm Island project features small islands that are shaped out of Sheikh Mohammed's poetry.

CINEMA

The Emirati film industry has been slow to develop, but not for a lack of talent. 2005 saw the premiere of the country's first feature film, *Al Hilm* (The Dream) a light-hearted lost-in-the-desert flick by Hani al-Shaibhani, following some quality short films and videos produced by local communications students. Disappointingly there have been no great follow-ups to Hani's in the way of feature films. The UAE now has two film festivals. Dubai local Masoud Amralla Al Ali's excellent Emirates Film Competition (held in Abu Dhabi) can be given credit for nurturing local talent

DUBAI ON SCREEN

> *Syriana* – Stephen Soderburgh (USA, 2005)
> *Code 46* – Michael Winterbottom (UK, 2004)
> *Dubai* – Rory B Quintos (Phillipines, 2005)
> *Dubai Return* – Aditya Bhattacharyya (India, 2005)
> *Al Hilm/The Dream* – Hani al-Shaibhani (UAE, 2005)

DUBAI SOUNDTRACK

> *Arabian Nights Vol 2: Club & Chillout Classics* -- an exotic compilation of Arabian-inspired chillout music, featuring Lemonada and other local sounds
> *Blue Bedouin* -- Hussain Al Bagali's blissful beats from the Dubai desert
> *The Desert Lounge Vol 1 & 2* -- taking inspiration from Hotel Costes et al, this is Madinat Jumeirah's 'musical evocation' of the mesmerising complex
> *Lemonada, The Arabian Latin Chillout Experience* -- Ahmad Ghannoum's Arab fusion meets Bossa Nova
> *Oryx* -- Dubaian expats combine ambient Arabian instrumentals, electronic dance and Arabic chants

through cash awards, while the more glamorous Dubai International Film Festival, which screens content from around the world, waited until its third year in 2006 to host a local film competition. The Emirati entries screened were underwhelming, unfortunately, but while media attention continued to focus on Hollywood stars imported for the festival, there were some outstanding films screened from around the Middle East.

DANCE & SONG

Traditional Emirati folk music and dances are performed at weddings and social gatherings. Brought to the Gulf by East African slaves, the *liwa* is danced to a loud drumbeat, and traditionally sung in Swahili. A typical Bedouin dance celebrating courage, strength and unity, the *ayyalah* is performed throughout the Gulf. Visitors can see traditional dance and music during Dubai Shopping Festival and on National Day, performed at the Heritage Village in the evenings. Interesting contemporary Arab music from collectives such as Oryx, Blue Bedouin and Lemonada has been produced at Dubai Media City. The fusion of sounds is often the result of the diverse backgrounds of the musicians. While some Arabian bands perform everything from metal to punk, the music you're most likely to hear on the radio is *khaleeji*, the traditional Gulf style recognisable to those familiar with Arabic pop music.

DIRECTORY
TRANSPORT
ARRIVAL & DEPARTURE
AIR

Dubai International Airport (Map p42-3, D8; ☎ general inquiries 224 5555, flight inquiries 206 6666; www.dubaiairport.com) is the busiest in the Middle East and is rightly renowned for its excellent duty-free shopping. All major international airlines use Terminal 1, the main terminal; other carriers use the much smaller Terminal 2. There are left-luggage facilities at the airport.

Getting To and From the Airport

The airport is about 5km south-east of the city centre. **Airport buses** (☎ 800 4848) run every 30 minutes to Deira (bus 401) and Bur Dubai (bus 402), and the fare is Dh3. If you're staying at one of the beach hotels, it's worth checking if your hotel has a free service to the airport. The easiest option is to take one of the Dubai Transport taxis from the arrivals area. A ride to the Deira souq area is about Dh35, Bur Dubai around Dh45, while to the Jumeirah hotels fares cost around Dh60, depending on the amount of traffic chaos.

TRAVEL DOCUMENTS

To enter Dubai your passport must have at least six months' validity from the date of your arrival. Officially, you will be denied entry if your passport shows any evidence of travel to Israel, and Israeli passport holders are not permitted to enter.

VISAS

Visas valid for 60 days are available on arrival for citizens of most developed countries but many of these are currently under review as some countries have not extended the same courtesy to

CLIMATE CHANGE & TRAVEL

Travel – especially air travel – is a significant contributor to global climate change. At Lonely Planet, we believe that all who travel have a responsibility to limit their personal impact. As a result, we have teamed with Rough Guides and other concerned industry partners to support Climate Care, which allows people to offset the greenhouse gases they are responsible for with contributions to energy-saving projects and other climate-friendly initiatives in the developing world. Lonely Planet offsets all staff and author travel.

For more information, turn to the responsible travel pages on www.lonelyplanet.com. For details on offsetting your carbon emissions and a carbon calculator, go to www.climatecare.org.

UAE citizens. Check the situation before travelling. These include all western European countries, Australia, Brunei, Canada, Hong Kong, Japan, Malaysia, New Zealand, Singapore, South Korea and the USA. No fee is charged for tourist visas. Citizens of other Gulf Cooperative Council (GCC) countries do not need visas to enter the UAE.

For citizens of any other countries, a transit or tourist visa must be arranged before travelling through a sponsor. This can be a hotel, a company or a resident of the UAE. Most hotels charge at least Dh200 to arrange a visa.

GETTING AROUND

The best way of getting around Dubai is by taxi, unless you're reading this after December 2008 when Dubai's monorail is expected to commence operating. Only hire a car if you are a confident driver who can handle Middle East traffic madness and you plan on taking a couple of day trips. Nonresidents intending to drive in the UAE should make sure they have an international drivers licence. While there is a public bus system, slowly melting into a bus-stop seat in 40°C heat is not a great way to experience Dubai. Note that only major roads have names in Dubai – all minor roads have a confusing system of numbers that begin all over again in each neighbourhood area.

TAXI

Dubai has a large, modern fleet of metered taxis, however the driving skills and knowledge of the city inhabited by the guy behind the wheel varies wildly. The starting fare is Dh3 plus Dh1.43 per kilometre, rising to Dh3.50 plus Dh1.70 per kilometre between 10pm and 6am. Drivers will try to round up to the nearest Dh5, so keep some smaller notes (Dh5s and Dh10s) and coins handy. **Dubai Transport** (☎ 208 0808) can provide wheelchair-accessible taxis if you book in advance. Note that unmarked (and often unmetered) limousines offered by many hotels often charge double normal taxis. If you are offered one of these, you can politely refuse and ask for a normal taxi. Don't believe them if they tell you the price is the same because it's not.

CAR

If you're planning on taking a day or overnight excursion from Dubai, hiring a car is the best way to do it, though traffic congestion in Dubai can be a real problem at peak hours (roughly 7am to 10am and 4.30pm to 7pm). Parking is plentiful and petrol is sold by the gallon (just over 4.5L). Regular petrol costs Dh4 per gallon and premium is Dh4.56.

BUS

Dubai's **Roads and Transport Authority** (RTA; ☎ 800 9090; www.rta.ae) runs an extensive city bus network, predominantly used by guest workers (although an increasing number of budget travellers are giving this a go). As a result, women travelling solo may feel uncomfortable – it's best to sit in the women's section at the front of the bus to avoid harassment. From the main bus stations on Al-Ghubaiba Rd in Bur Dubai or Al-Khor St in Deira you'll be able to catch a bus to most destinations in the city. Fares range from Dh1 to Dh3.50 and services are frequent. Numbers and routes are posted on the buses in English and Arabic.

ABRA

Dubai's **Roads and Transport Authority** (RTA; ☎ 800 9090; www.rta.ae) also runs the city's wonderful *abra* (water taxi) service. To cross the creek costs Dh1 (pay on the boat) and there are three set routes that run between the following *abra* stations: route 1 leaves Deira from the Deira Old Souq station and goes to the Bur Dubai station near the Bank of Baroda; route 2 leaves Deira from Al-Sabkha station and goes to the Bur Dubai Old Souq station in Bur Dubai; the new route 3 leaves the brand spanking new Baniyas station near Arbift Tower and Dubai Municipality

and goes to the new Al-Seef Abra station. All of these are ideally positioned for creek walks. The *abras* function from early morning till midnight. You can also hire one from any of the stations to do your own tour of the Creek for a standard rate of Dh100 per hour.

PRACTICALITIES

BUSINESS HOURS

Government departments generally work from Sunday to Thursday, 7.30am to 2.30pm, and private companies generally open for business from 8am to 5pm or from 9am to 6pm. The weekend is Friday – the weekly Muslim holy day – and Saturday. Shopping malls are generally open 10am to 10pm and other shops from around 10am to 1pm and 4pm to 9pm, give or take half an hour to an hour. On Fridays most shops are shut in the morning and open around 2pm.

ELECTRICITY

British-style three-pin wall sockets are used, but most appliances sold in Dubai have the European two-pin plug configuration. Adaptors are inexpensive and available everywhere. Try Carrefour or the nearest neighbourhood supermarket.

Voltage 220V
Frequency 50Hz
Cycle AC
Plugs British-style 3-pin

ISLAMIC HOLIDAYS

Hejira Year	New Year	Prophet's Birthday	Ramadan	Eid al-Fitr	Eid al-Adha
1428	20.01.07	31.03.07	13.09.07	13.10.07	20.12.07
1429	10.01.08	20.03.08	02.09.08	01.10.08	08.12.08
1430	29.12.08	09.03.09	22.08.09	21.09.09	28.11.09

HOLIDAYS

Fixed holiday dates in Dubai are New Year's Day (1 January), Accession Day (of HH Sheikh Zayed, 6 August) and National Day (2 December). Religious holidays follow the Islamic lunar calendar and approximate dates are listed, but the exact dates are determined by the sighting of the moon. Eid al-Fitr is a three-day celebration after Ramadan (p29), and Eid al-Adha is a four-day celebration after the main pilgrimage to Mecca, or Hajj.

INTERNET

Most hotels offer internet access to their guests, with broadband and wi-fi fast becoming the norm. For those travelling with wi-fi equipped laptops or PDAs, Etisalat (the UAE's main service provider) has an iZone wi-fi service. Wherever you see the iZone logo you can buy prepaid cards (starting at Dh15 for one hour) and start wireless surfing. Most shopping centres and Starbucks cafés have iZone.

There are a few specialist internet cafés around the city, and you'll find small cafés in the shopping centres that have terminals. Rates are around Dh10 to Dh15 per hour and reliable internet cafés include:

Al-Jalssa Internet Café (Map p56-7, D2; ☎ 351 4617; Al-Ain Shopping Centre, Al-Mankhool Rd; ☼ 9am-1am)

French Connection (Map p72-3, G4; ☎ 343 8311; Wafa Tower, Sheikh Zayed Rd; ☼ 9am-1am)

Some useful websites:

7 Days (www.7days.ae) Online version of the UAE newspaper with the most amusing letters to the editor section.

Dubai Tourism & Commerce Marketing (www.dubaitourism.ae) The official tourism website.

Sheikh Mohammed bin Rashid al-Maktoum (www.sheikhmohammed.com) The main man's own website.

UAE Interact (www.uaeinteract.com) The official Ministry of Information and Culture website – much more interesting than it sounds.

LANGUAGE

Arabic is the official language, but English is the language you'll generally hear most – as well as a bit of Hindi, Urdu and Farsi. Signs are nearly always in both Arabic and English. While it's great to learn some easy phrases in Arabic (much appreciated by Emiratis), it's worth remembering that most people you'll deal with might not speak the language.

BASICS

Hello/Welcome.	*marHaba*
Greetings (Peace be upon you).	*al-salaam alaykum*
(response) Peace be upon you.	*wa alaykum es-salaam*
Goodbye.	*ma'al salaama*
How are you?	*kay fahlak?*
Good, thanks.	*zein, shukran*
Excuse me.	*ismalee*
Yes.	*na'am*
No.	*la*
Thank you (very much).	*shukran (jazeelan)*
You're welcome.	*afwan*
Do you speak English?	*titkallam ingleezi?*
I don't understand.	*ana la afham*
How much is this?	*bcham hatha?*
That's too expensive.	*ghaalee jidan*

EATING & DRINKING

Do you have vegetarian dishes?	*haal indaak akl nabati laahm?*
That was delicious!	*kan al-aak l lazeez*
Please bring the bill.	*'ateenee il-kaa 'ima min fadlak*
breakfast	*futtoor*
lunch	*ghadha*
dinner	*asha*

EMERGENCIES

It's an emergency!	*Halet isa'af!*
Call the police!	*etasell bil shurta!*
Call an ambulance!	*etasell bil sayyaret al-isa'af!*
Call a doctor!	*etasell bil tabeeb!*
I'm sick.	*ana maareed*
Help!	*moosaai'd!*

DAYS & NUMBERS

today	*al-yom*
tomorrow	*baachir*
yesterday	*il-baarih*
0	*sifr*
1	*waHid*
2	*ithneen*
3	*thalatha*
4	*arba'a*
5	*khamsa*
6	*sitta*
7	*sab'a*
8	*thimania*
9	*tis'a*
10	*ashra*

11	*Hda'ash*
12	*thna'ash*
13	*thalathta'ash*
20	*'ishreen*
21	*waHid wa 'ishreen*
30	*thalatheen*
40	*arbi'een*
50	*khamseen*
60	*sitteen*
70	*saba'een*
80	*thimaneen*
90	*tis'een*
100	*imia*
101	*imia waHid*
102	*imia wa-ithneen*
103	*imia wa-thalatha*
200	*imiatain*
300	*thalatha imia*
1000	*alf*

COMMUNICATIONS

I want to buy a (phone card).
  ana areed ashtaree (beetaget Hatef/kart telefon)
I want to make a call (to…)
  ana areed an atsell (bee…)
I want to make a reverse-charge/collect call.
  ana areed taHweel kulfet al-mukalama ila al-mutagee
Where's the local internet café?
  wayn magHa al-internet?
Where can I find a/an…?
  wayn mumkin an ajed…?
I'd like a/an…
  ana areed…
    adaptor plug
      aakhaz tawseel

charger for my phone
  shaHen leel Hatef
mobile/cell phone for hire
  mobail ('mobile') leel ajar
prepaid mobile/cell phone
  mobail moos baq aldaf '
SIM card for your network
  seem kart lee shabaket al-itsalaat

HEALTH

Where's the nearest…?
  wayn aghrab…?

chemist	*saydalee*
(night)	*(laylee)*
doctor	*tabeeb*
hospital	*mustashfa*

I have (a)…
  ana andee…

diarrhoea	*is-haal*
fever	*sukhoona*
headache	*suda or waja' ras*
pain	*alam/waja'*

MONEY

The UAE dirham (Dh) is divided into 100 fils. Notes are available in denominations of Dh5, 10, 20, 50, 100, 200, 500 and 1000. There are Dh1, 50 fils, 25 fils, 10 fils and 5 fils coins (the latter two are rarely used). The coins only show the denomination in Arabic, so it is a great way to learn.

EXCHANGE RATES

The UAE dirham is fully convertible and – for better or worse depending on where you're coming from – pegged to the US dollar at a rate of Dh3.6725. Exchange rates are better in the city than at the airport. Check the latest exchange rates at www.xe.com/ucc.

Australia	A$1	Dh3.10
Canada	C$1	Dh3.43
Euro	€1	Dh4.94
New Zealand	NZ$1	Dh2.81
South Africa	ZAR1	Dh0.51
UK	£1	Dh7.34
USA	US$1	Dh3.67

COSTS

Although Dubai built its reputation as a luxury holiday destination, shoe-stringers can get by on Dh200 a day by staying at the youth hostel or a gold souq one-star, eating shwarmas and in cheap eateries, walking everywhere in winter, or taking the *abras* and buses everywhere the rest of the time. Business and leisure travellers can look at spending anything upwards of Dh1200 (eg starting at Dh700 with a corporate rate at a good four-star deluxe, Dh150 for lunch, Dh50 for return taxi around the city, and Dh250 for dinner). Meals can vary from Dh60 for two in a cheap Arabic eatery (no alcohol) to Dh500 for two, which includes a bottle of wine in a fine restaurant.

NEWSPAPERS & MAGAZINES

There are many English-language daily newspapers available in Dubai. The best is the recently launched *Emirates Today*, but most local papers feel more Mumbai than Dubai and thankfully newsagents also stock some international newspapers. Locally produced glossies include *Alef*, *Viva*, *Grazia* and *Emirates Woman*, and you can check out Dubai's celebrities in *Ahlan!* entertainment magazine. The weekly *Time Out Dubai* has decent listings on upcoming events, as does the monthly *What's On*.

ORGANISED TOURS

Plenty of organised tours will see you stuck in traffic, so we suggest that you take to the skies with either a helicopter tour or a gentler balloon ride. **Heli Dubai** (☎ 224 4033; www.helidubai.com) offers myriad trips including landing at the Burj Al Arab heli pad (definitely quite an experience) as well as checking out the offshore Palm and The World projects. A little more tranquil is a trip with **Balloon Adventures** (☎ 273 8585; www.ballooning.ae), which offers sunrise tours (during the cooler months) over the dunes with views of the rugged Hajj mountains.

PHOTOGRAPHY & VIDEO

Dubai is a technology-crazed city, so there are memory cards and other accessories for digital cameras on just about every corner. The UAE uses the PAL video system.

TELEPHONE

The UAE's main telecommunications system is run by the state telecommunications company, **Etisalat** (Map p56-7, D2; cnr Baniyas & Omar ibn al-Khattab Rds; 24hr). Local calls from residences in Dubai are free (excluding mobile calls). Public phones are mostly card phones, and phonecards (Dh30 and Dh60) are sold at grocery shops and supermarkets – don't buy them from street vendors.

Mobile phones are the de facto standard in Dubai – when giving someone your number it's assumed that it's for a mobile not a fixed line. Dubai's mobile system is GSM, and roaming agreements exist with many other countries. Etisalat's mobile numbers begin with 050 in the UAE. The country's new service provider, Du (www .du.ae) uses a 055 prefix for its mobile phones.

Visitors can buy a prepaid wasel (sim) card for Dh165 from the airport and Etisalat offices, which can be recharged with a prepaid mobile charge card, in denomina-

tions of Dh25 and Dh40, available from most supermarkets and grocery stores. Etisalat also offers a special package called Ahlan for short-term visitors. It costs Dh90 for 90 days and includes 90 minutes of talk time, 9 SMS messages, missed call notifications, call waiting, and your first overseas call for free.

Useful telephone numbers

Dubai Area Code ☎ 04
Etisalat Mobile Code ☎ 050
Directory Inquiries ☎ 181
International Operator ☎ 100
UAE Country Code ☎ 971

TIPPING

Tips are not generally expected in restaurants, as a service charge is added to your bill, though this goes to the restaurant, not the waiter. If you want to leave a tip, 10% is ample. Taxi drivers will make a vague attempt to give you change, but have already mentally rounded up your fare to the nearest Dh5. Valets, hotel porters and the like will expect and appreciate a tip of Dh2 and upwards.

TOURIST INFORMATION

The official tourism board of the Dubai government is the **Department of Tourism & Commerce Marketing** (DTCM; ☎ 223 0000; www.dubaitourism .ae). As well as the main welcome

DIRECTORY

bureaus listed below, most of Dubai's shopping malls have tourism desks with maps and information.

Airport (Map p42-3, D8; ☎ 224 5252/224 4098; Dubai International Airport; ⏱ 24hr)

Baniyas Square (Map p42-3, B2; ☎ 228 5000; Baniyas Sq; ⏱ 9am-11pm)

TRAVELLERS WITH DISABILITIES

Once outside the airport (which has decent facilities), Dubai is not a particularly disabled-friendly destination. **Dubai Transport** (☎ 208 0808) has taxis that can take wheelchairs. New hotels generally have at least a couple of rooms that have good or excellent disabled access and facilities, as do some of the hotel restaurants.

>INDEX

See also separate subindexes for See (p158), Shop (p158), Eat (p159), Drink (p160) and Play (p160).

⊙ SEE

⌂ SHOP

000 map pages